CORPUS-DRIVEN
CDV
VOCABULARY

NAN'UN-DO ENGLISH VOCABULARY for ACADEMIC PURPOSES　南雲堂 学問別 重要英単語シリーズ

VOCABULARY for LAW

JOHN P. RACINE　TAKAYUKI NAKANISHI

NAN'UN-DO

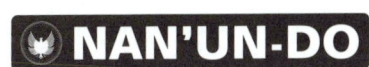

学問別　重要英単語：法学

Vocabulary for Law

Copyright © 2016

by

John P. Racine

and

Takayuki Nakanishi

All rights reserved.

No part of this book may be reproduced in any form without written permission
from the authors and Nan'un-do Co., Ltd.

Acknowledgments

The authors wish to thank Takuya Matsumoto, Yuki Shimizu, Ayumi 'Kuro' Sasaki, and Haruka Aoki for their assistance in gathering data for the corpus from which these materials were derived. Thanks also to Yutaka Tajima and Noriko Ofuji.

はしがき

　この本は10ユニットで構成され，それぞれのユニットには法律と法学に関連する30単語が含まれています。各ユニットの終わりには2つのクイズが用意されていますので，次のユニットに進む前に理解度をテストしてみてください。

　それぞれの単語の記述は，次の情報を含んでいます。

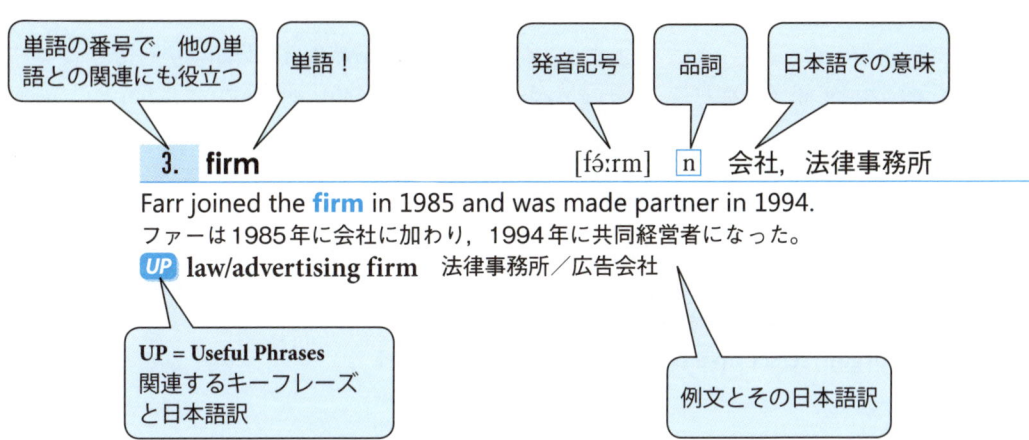

　それぞれの単語は，あなたの分野に関連あるものが選ばれています。つまり，法学の学生に必要不可欠な単語ということです。実際，この本の最初に出てくる単語は，繰り返し例文の中で何度も取り上げられていることに気づくと思います。これは，それらの単語があなたの分野において，いかに重要であるかを示しています。同時に，繰り返し出てくることで，より簡単に覚えることができます。そして同じ単語により多く触れることで，より速く覚えることもできるのです。

　語彙について，教師および研究者たちは現在，単語知識に関しては，単語の意味を単に知ること以上に多くのことがあると分かっています。それぞれの単語が文脈の中で使用される方法を認識することも非常に重要です。それゆえ，例文は現実世界での実用的な単語の使用を基本としています。文脈の中でそれぞれの単語が使用されているのを見ながら学習することで，英語を話したり，書いたりする時の能力の向上につながります。

　もしある単語が一般的に2つ以上の形（例えば，名詞，および動詞として）で使用されているなら，両方の形を網羅しています（ 14. appeal を参照）。一方で，もしある単語が形を変えずに違う意味を持っている場合は，それらは例文で別々に提示しています（ 9. justice を参照）。

学習を進めていると，日本語の意味に色が付けられた箇所があるので注意してください。それらは，その単語を学習する際に助けとなる重要な情報です。例えば，次の例の "file" という名詞の意味を知っているかもしれません。しかし，ここの強調された箇所は，さらに動詞としても使用できることを教えてくれます。

13. file　　　　　　　　　　　[fáɪl]　 v 　提起する
The court decided that the case **filed** against the company will be allowed to move forward.
法廷は，会社に対して提起された訴訟を進めることを認めると決定した。
 file charges/a case　訴訟を起こす

下記の例では， Check! も表示されています。これは， **65. commission** の単語に戻って見直すべきであることを意味しています。なぜなら，これらの2つの単語が言語的に関連があるからです。単語間の言語関係を認識することは，単語知識および語彙力を増やす素晴らしい方法です。

85. committee　　　　　　[kəmíti]　 n 　委員，委員会
 I have served on the banking **committee** for eight years.
私は，8年間銀行委員を務めた。
　　　　　 UP organize/set up a committee　委員会を組織する

本全体にわたるもう1つの特徴は ポイント! です。これは，それぞれの分野における単語，もしくはその使用法を理解するのを助けるための重要な追加情報です。下記の例では，"act" という単語の一般的な例があります。しかし ポイント! は，法学に関係する専門的な使い方もあることを教えてくれます。ポイント! の中の説明は，基礎単語知識の構築を助けてくれます。

15. act　　　　　　　　　　　[ǽkt]　 n 　法律，法，行為
She had to pay $500 under Section 3(1) of the Dangerous Dogs **Act** 1991 after her dog bit two boys.
彼女は，飼い犬が2人の少年達に噛み付いたので，1991年に施行された危険犬種法の3条1項によって，500ドルを払わなければならなかった。

ポイント！ 法的用語の場合，大文字になる。小文字の場合は，人の行為を表す。

ユニットの終りごとに，メモをとれる **Vocabulary Notes** があります。そこに書かれたアドバイスをもとに自由に学習に役立ててください。そして，学習した単語についての理解度をチェックするための2つのセルフテスト（**Test Yourself**）があります。**Quiz 1** は，学習した単語の意味をどの程度理解しているかについてのテストです。**Quiz 2** は，学習した単語を使用する能力をテストするものです。答えは，62ページにあります。

How to Use This Book

This book is comprised of 10 units of 30 words each. After the word entries, you'll see a *Vocabulary Notes* sections for you to take notes while studying, and two quizzes so you can test yourself before beginning the next unit.

Each word entry includes the following information:

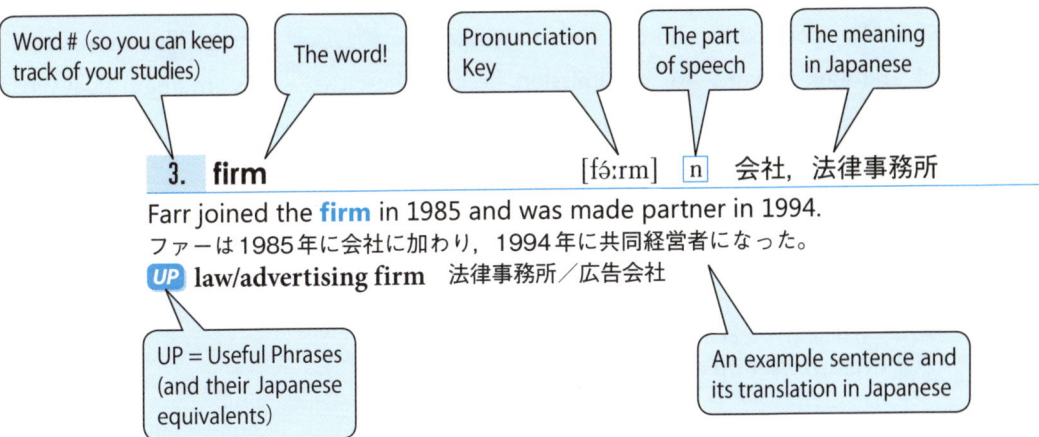

Each word has been selected for its relevance to your field. That is, each word is an essential word for students of law. In fact, you will notice that words that appear near the beginning of the book will come up again and again in subsequent example sentences. This shows how centrally important these words are to you and your studies. At the same time, this will make them easier to remember. The more exposure you have to them, the more quickly and easily you'll remember them.

Vocabulary teachers and researchers now know that there is a lot more to *word knowledge* than just knowing the meaning of the word. It is vitally important to recognize the way words are used in context. For that reason, each example sentence is based on the word's real use in the real world. Learning the words while seeing them in context will also strengthen your ability to use them in speech and writing.

If a word is commonly used in more than one form (e.g., as a noun and as a verb) both forms will be listed (see 14. **appeal**). If there are more than one meaning for the same form of the word (for example, two different nouns), those will be listed separately with their own example sentences (see 9. **justice**).

While you are studying, watch out for the highlighted areas in certain entries, like in 13. below. These are designed to draw your attention to important information that will help you to learn the word. For example, you may know the meaning of the noun *file* already, but the highlight here tells you that it can also be used as a verb.

13. file [fáɪl] [v] 提起する
The court decided that the case **filed** against the company will be allowed to move forward.
法廷は，会社に対して提起された訴訟を進めることを認めると決定した。
 file charges/a case　訴訟を起こす

The entry for 85. **committee** shown below illustrates the ⊖ *Check!* feature. This means that you should go back and look at word 65. **commission**, because these two words are linguistically related. Recognizing the connections between words is a great way to increase your word knowledge and your vocabulary power.

85. committee [kəmíti] [n] 委員，委員会
　I have served on the banking **committee** for eight years.
　　　私は，8年間銀行委員を務めた。
　　　organize/set up a committee　委員会を組織する

Another important feature of this book is the ポイント! box, shown in 15. below. The ポイント! box provides important information to help you understand the word or its usage in your area of study. These explanations will allow you to build on your basic word knowledge.

15. act [ǽkt] [n] 法律，法，行為
She had to pay $500 under Section 3(1) of the Dangerous Dogs **Act** 1991 after her dog bit two boys.
彼女は，飼い犬が2人の少年達に噛み付いたので，1991年に施行された危険犬種法の3条1項によって，500ドルを払わなければならなかった。

ポイント!　法的用語の場合，大文字になる。小文字の場合は，人の行為を表す。

At the end of each unit is the **Vocabulary Notes** space where you can take notes as you study. There are also two self-tests to check your understanding of the words. **Quiz 1** tests your understanding of the meaning of the words. **Quiz 2** tests your ability to use the words in sentences.

Enjoy your studies!

Contents

はしがき .... Ⅲ

How to Use This Book .... Ⅴ

Unit 1 8

Unit 2 13

Unit 3 18

Unit 4 23

Unit 5 28

Unit 6 33

Unit 7 38

Unit 8 43

Unit 9 48

Unit 10 53

Vocabulary Notebook 58

Index 60

Test Yourself – Answer Key 62

Unit 1

1. case　　　[kéɪs]　n　判例（訴訟の意味で使用されることも多い）主張（言い分），事件

This was a losing **case** for the government.
これは，政府にとって勝ち目のない訴訟だった。
UP criminal/civil case　刑事事件／民事事件

2. judge　　　[dʒʌ́dʒ]　n　裁判官

We need more education and training for **judges** in the U.S. and abroad.
米国や海外で裁判官のための，より多くの教育と訓練が必要である。
UP presiding judge　裁判長

3. firm　　　[fə́ːrm]　n　会社，法律事務所

Farr joined the **firm** in 1985 and was made partner in 1994.
ファーは1985年に会社に加わり，1994年に共同経営者になった。
UP law/advertising firm　法律事務所／広告会社

4. claim　　　[kléɪm]　v　主張する，訴える

The university **claims** its policy falls within the guidelines of the judge's decision.
大学は，その方針が，裁判官が決定した指針に適うと主張している。
UP claim responsibility/victory　責任を主張する／勝利を主張する

5. rule　　　[rúːl]　v　判決する，決定を下す

A judge **ruled** last year that she didn't owe the money.
裁判官は，彼女には支払いの義務がないと昨年判決した。

ruling　　　[rúːlɪŋ]　n　判決

In his **ruling** last week, Judge Hellerstein said Whitley hadn't gotten a fair trial.
先週の判決において，ヘラースティン裁判官は，ウィトリーが公正に裁かれていなかったと述べた。
UP unanimous ruling　満場一致の判決

 この単語は，法的には動詞として使用することが多い。

6. legal　　　[líːg(ə)l]　adj　法的な

Chen provided **legal** advice to the disabled on how to protect their rights.
チェンは，障害者の権利を守る方法について法的な助言を障害者に行った。
UP legal system　法のシステム

7. issue　　　[íʃuː, ísjuː]　v　下す（目的語が「判決」や「決定」の場合）

On Monday, the court **issued** its decision in the closely-watched case.
月曜日に，法廷は注意深く検証していた訴訟に判決を下した。

　　　n　争点，問題

This has become a top legal **issue** for the nation's business community.
これは，国の経済界における最大の法的な争点となった。
UP bring up/raise an issue　問題を取り上げる

8

8. attorney [ətə́ːni | ətə́ː-] n 弁護士

You have the right to speak to an **attorney**.
あなたは，弁護士と話す権利を有している。
UP district/defense attorney　地方検事／被告側の弁護士

 アメリカにおいて主に使用する。イギリスでは barrister（法廷弁士）または，solicitor（事務弁護士）という。それら3つとも lawyer ということもできる。

9. justice [dʒʌ́stɪs] n 正義

I hope that this conviction offers his family some sense of **justice**.
この有罪判決が彼の家族に何らかの正義をもたらすことを願う。

n 最高裁判事

Justice Alito said that such costs were not the court's concern.
アリット最高裁判事は，そのような経費は法廷が関与する事ではないと言った。

n 司法

The Prime Minister warned Libya that international **justice** has a long reach and a long memory.
首相はリビアに対し，国際司法の及ぶ範囲は広範であり，記憶も永く残ると警告した。
UP administer/dispense justice　法を施行する

 肩書，敬称は大文字で始まる。

10. federal [fédərəl, -drəl] adj 連邦の

They put pressure on him to drop the **federal** cases.
彼らは，連邦の訴訟を取り下げるよう，彼に圧力をかけた。
UP federal government/court　連邦政府／連邦裁判所

11. partner [pɑ́ɚtnɚ | pɑ́ːtnə] n 共同経営者

She has several years of experience as a law firm **partner**.
彼女は法律事務所の共同経営者としての経験が数年ある。
UP junior/senior partner　下級の共同経営者／上級の共同経営者

12. trial [tráɪəl] n 裁判，公判

Judges will either accept the request or send the case to **trial**.
裁判官は申立てを受け入れるか，訴訟を裁判にかける。
UP conduct/hold a trial　裁判を行う

13. file [fáɪl] v 提起する

The court decided that the case **filed** against the company will be allowed to move forward.
法廷は，会社に対して提起された訴訟の進行を認めると決定した。
UP file charges/a case　訴訟を起こす

14. appeal [əpíːl] v 控訴する，上訴する

The woman's lawyer **appealed** the decision.
その女性の弁護士は，判決に対し控訴した。

n 控訴，上訴

If an **appeal** is made, we will oppose it.
上訴が行われれば，我々はそれに対抗する。
UP file/lodge an appeal　控訴する

Unit 1

15. act [ǽkt] [n] 法律，法，行為

She had to pay $500 under Section 3(1) of the Dangerous Dogs **Act** 1991 after her dog bit two boys.
彼女は，飼い犬が2人の少年達に噛み付いたので，1991年に施行された危険犬種法の3条1項によって，500ドルを払わなければならなかった。

> ポイント！ 法的用語の場合，大文字になる。小文字の場合は，人の行為を表す。

16. client [kláɪənt] [n] 依頼人

The lawyer said his **client** would appeal.
弁護士は，依頼人が上訴するだろうと言った。
UP potential/prospective client　潜在的な依頼人

17. charge [tʃάərdʒ | tʃάːdʒ] [v] 告発する

The 29-year-old was **charged** with leaving the scene of an accident.
その29歳の者は，事故現場を去ったとして告発された。

[n] 告発

The federal government will bring **charges** against his client.
連邦政府は，依頼人を相手取って訴訟を起こすだろう。
UP bring/lay/press charges　刑事訴訟を起こす

18. security [sɪkjʊ́(ə)rəti] [n] 警備，安全，安全保障

The company's goal is to improve aviation safety and **security**.
その会社の目標は，航空技術の安全性と安全確保である。
UP ensure/provide security　安全を保障する／安全を提供する

19. party [pάərti | pάː-] [n] 当事者（訴訟当事者をさすことが多い）

The justices ordered the **parties** to address that issue.
裁判官は，両当事者にその問題について述べるよう命じた。
UP guilty/innocent party　犯人／無実の人

20. seek [síːk] [v] ～しようとする，～を求める

Lawyers for the musician are **seeking** to argue his case in court.
その音楽家の弁護士は，裁判所でその事件を審理することを求めている。
UP seek help/advice　助けを求める

21. practice [prǽktɪs] [v] 法実務を行う，業とする

While in law school, I dreamed about **practicing** international law.
ロースクールにいた時，国際法を扱う弁護士になることを夢見ていた。
UP practice law/medicine　法実務を行う／（医者が）開業している

22. plaintiff [pléɪntɪf] [n] 原告

He was unable to respond to the **plaintiff**'s legal arguments.
彼は，原告の法的主張に答えることができなかった。
UP find for the plaintiff　原告に勝訴を認定する

> ポイント！ defendant は，被告。最近では「原告」は claimant を用いることもある。

Vocabulary for Law

23. authority [əθɔ́rəti, ɔː-, -θɑ́ɾ-ɹ- | ɔːθɔ́r-, ə-] [n] 当局，（関係機関）

Authorities said several people had been shot.
当局は，数人が撃たれたと言った。
UP local/government authorities　地方当局／政府当局

 この単語は通常，例文にあるように複数形で使用される。

24. supreme court [sʊprím] [kɔ́ɚt | kɔ́ːt] [n] 最高裁判所

The **Supreme Court** has agreed to hear a federal appeals court case from California.
最高裁判所は，カリフォルニアの連邦高等裁判所の事件を審理することに同意した。

25. counsel [káʊnsl] [n] 弁護士（法律顧問）

Shortly before trial, Kelly was invited by lead **counsel** to handle the case.
ケリーは裁判の少し前に，主任弁護士から当該事件を扱うよう頼まれた。
UP counsel for the defense/prosecution　被告側弁護団／検察側弁護団

26. try [tráɪ] [v] 審理する

Check! 12. The case has to be **tried** in New Jersey if there is going to be a fair result.
公平な結果にしたいならば，その訴訟はニュージャージー州で審理されるべきである。
UP be tried as a juvenile/an adult　少年（少女）として審理される／大人として審理される

27. crime [kráɪm] [n] 犯罪

I want to help the police fight terrorist activity and **crime**.
私は，テロ活動や犯罪と闘う警察を支援したい。
UP commit a crime　犯罪を犯す

28. release [rɪlíːs] [v] 釈放する

Help get my wife **released** as soon as possible.
妻ができるだけ早く釈放されるよう助けてください。
UP released from jail/prison　刑務所から釈放された

29. statement [stéɪtmənt] [n] 声明書

His brother read a **statement** asking for his family to be given their privacy.
彼の兄は，家族のプライバシーを求める声明書を読んだ。
UP issue/make/release a statement　声明を出す

30. require [rɪkwáɪɚ | -kwáɪə] [v] 必要とする

Eighty-eight percent of the companies now **require** international legal advice.
企業の88パーセントは，現在国際法の助言を必要とする。
UP required by law　法によって必要とされた

Unit 1　11

Vocabulary Notes

_____
_____
_____
_____
_____
_____
_____
_____

Try saying new words out loud.

 # Unit 1 Test Yourself

Quiz 1: Match the words and phrases with their meanings.

1. issue   _____   a. 審理する
2. release   _____   b. 判決
3. charge   _____   c. 法実務を行う
4. practice   _____   d. 弁護士
5. ruling   _____   e. 争点
6. try   _____   f. 釈放する
7. counsel   _____   g. 告発する

Quiz 2: Fill in the blanks with the best word or phrase from this unit.

| firm | crime | clients | judge | required | supreme court | federal |

1. The law says that everyone in the car is _____ to wear a seatbelt.
2. Killing someone may be the most serious _____ in the world.
3. My business is in trouble because I don't have enough _____.
4. I want to become a lawyer and join a big law _____ in the future.
5. In many countries, the health insurance system is run by the _____ government.

Now check your answers on page 62.

12 *Vocabulary for Law*

Unit 2

31. criminal [krímənl] [adj] 刑事上の，犯罪の
The mother could face **criminal** charges for abandoning her child.
その母親は，子どもを遺棄した罪で刑事訴追されるかもしれない。

[Check! 27.] [n] 犯人，犯罪者
Police stepped up efforts to seize handguns from **criminals**.
警察は，犯人から拳銃を押収するために努力した。
UP criminal case/investigation　刑事事件／犯罪捜査

32. defendant [dɪféndənt] [n] 被告人
Minutes before the trial is due to start, the **defendant** is talking to counsel.
公判開始時刻の数分前，被告人は弁護人と話している。
UP find for the defendant　被告人に勝訴を認定する

33. evidence [évədns, -dèns | -dns] [n] 証拠
They began to collect **evidence** to use in court.
彼らは，裁判で使用する証拠を収集し始めた。
UP furnish/give/introduce evidence　証拠をそろえる／証拠を与える／証拠を提出する

> **ポイント!** この単語は常に単数形で，不可算となる。

34. involve [ɪnvάlv, -ɔ́ːlv | -ɔ́lv] [v] 関わる，伴う
This is an isolated issue and no other partner or member of staff was **involved**.
これは別件で，他のパートナー，またはスタッフの誰もが関わってはいなかった。
UP directly involved　直接関わる

35. policy [pάləsi | pɔ́l-] [n] 政策
The campaign has been focused on **policy** issues.
そのキャンペーンは，政策問題に焦点が置かれた。
UP adopt/establish a policy　政策を採択する／政策を立案する

36. fee [fíː] [n] 報酬
They were ordered to pay $1 million in attorney **fees**.
彼らは，弁護士報酬として100万ドルを払うよう命じられた。
UP pay/receive a fee　報酬を払う／報酬を受け取る

> **ポイント!** 使用される時は，例文のように複数形化されることが多い。

37. damages [dǽmədʒəz] [n] 損害賠償
The company has agreed to pay $25 million in **damages** to the Los Angeles businessman.
その企業は，ロサンゼルスの実業家に損害賠償として2,500万ドルを支払うことに同意した。
UP claim/sue for damages　損害賠償を請求する

> **ポイント!** 必ず複数形。

13

38. arrest [ərést] [v] 逮捕する

One person was **arrested** in connection with the attack.
ある人物が，攻撃に関与しているとして逮捕された。
UP place under arrest　人を拘禁する

39. area [é(ə)riə] [n] 分野，領域

You have expanded your skills and knowledge in an **area** to better serve your clients.
あなたは，依頼人の役に立つために，ある分野での技術と知識を広げた。
UP growth area　成長分野

40. sentence [séntəns, -tns | -təns] [v] 判決を宣告する

He was **sentenced** to nine years in prison.
彼は懲役9年の判決を宣告された。

[n] 刑

All prisoners are serving a **sentence** of more than one year in jail.
すべての囚人は，刑務所で1年以上の刑に服している。
UP give/impose a sentence　刑を申しわたす

41. comment [kɑ́ment | kɔ́m-] [v] 述べる，コメントする

The firm said that it was unable to **comment** on the case.
その会社は，訴訟についてコメントすることはできないと言った。

[n] 批評，見解，コメント

I've never received so many **comments** about a legal issue.
私はこれまで，法的な問題についてこれほど多くの批評を受けたことはなかった。
UP invite/solicit comments　コメントを求める

42. allege [əlédʒ] [v] 断言する，主張する，〜を理由として申し立てる

The memo **alleges** that Chang gave the senator many improper gifts of cash.
チャンが上院議員に不正な現金の贈答を何度も行ったと，メモは断定している。

alleged [əlédʒd, -ɪd] [adj] 申し立てられた，疑わしい

The report describes many **alleged** crimes during the First Congo War.
その記事は，第一次コンゴ戦争中に犯されたという多くの犯罪に光をあてている。
UP alleged victim/plot　疑わしい被害者／疑わしい計画

43. prosecutor [prɑ́sɪkjùːtɚ | prɔ́s-] [n] 検察官

A **prosecutor** said that Lohan cannot be released early.
検察官は，ローハンを早く釈放することはできないと言った。
UP federal prosecutor　連邦検察官

> **ポイント！** public prosecutor で公訴官（検察官）を意味し，アメリカでは district attorney が使用されることが多い。

44. lawsuit [lɔ́sùt] [n] 訴訟

In September 1998, they filed a **lawsuit** against the City of Chicago alleging discrimination.
1998年9月，彼らは差別を理由にシカゴ市を相手取り，訴訟を起こした。
UP bring/file a lawsuit　訴訟を起こす

> **ポイント！** この単語は，単純に suit という形で使用されることも多い。専門家の間では，「訴訟」は action を用いる場合もある。

14　*Vocabulary for Law*

45. process [práses, próʊ- | próʊ-] [n] 過程

The comments may have had an effect on public perception of the sentencing **process**.
そのコメントは，判決に至るまでの過程について，公衆の認識に影響を及ぼしたかもしれない。
UP judicial/legal process　司法の過程／法の過程

専門用語で process は，「裁判書類（訴状）」を意味することがある。

46. litigation [lìtəgéɪʃən] [n] 訴訟

"**Litigation** against those companies is now likely," he added.
彼は，「現在それらの会社に対して訴えを提起することもありうる」と付け加えた。
UP initiate/start litigation　訴訟を起こす

47. document [dákjʊmənt | dɔ́k-] [n] 文書

She said the letter was not a public **document** and declined to comment further.
彼女は，その手紙は公的な文書ではないと言い，それ以上コメントすることを拒否した。
UP legal/court documents　法律文書／法廷文書

document は，evidence（証拠）であり，「書証」と訳す。

48. drug [drʌ́g] [n] 薬物（ドラッグ）

The rate of illegal **drug** use rose last year to the highest level in nearly a decade.
昨年の違法な薬物の使用率は，約10年の中で最も高い割合にまで増加した。
UP take/do drugs　薬物に手を出す

この単語は，薬局で売っているような普通の薬を意味することもある。薬物のような違法物質を表す場合は，定冠詞なしの複数形で使用されることが多い。

49. fund [fʌ́nd] [n] 資金，財源

BP says the figure does not include a $20 billion **fund** for Gulf damages.
その数字は，メキシコ湾被害のための200億ドルの資金は含まないとBPは言う。
UP establish/set up a fund　資金を設ける

50. financial [fɪnǽnʃəl, faɪ-] [adj] 財政の

According to Bayer's **financial** statements, there were 1,450 lawsuits as of July 12.
ベイヤーの財政報告書によると，7月12日の時点で訴訟は1,450件だった。
UP financial aid/support　財政援助／財政サポート

51. defense [dɪféns] [n] 被告側，弁護

Check! 32.
Opening statements were made by a prosecutor and three **defense** attorneys.
冒頭陳述は，検事と3人の被告側弁護人によって行われた。
UP weak/strong defense　弱い弁護／強い弁護

スペルの違いは，defense はアメリカ英語で defence はイギリス英語となる。

Unit 2　15

52. bill   [bíl] [n] 法案

The **bill** could be voted on again later this month.
その法案が今月末に再議決されるかもしれない。
UP introduce/propose a bill　法案を提出する

53. v   [prep] 対

The case of United States **v** Turner was assigned to Judge Walter.
アメリカ合衆国対ターナーの裁判は、ウォルター判事に割り当てられた。

 これは versus の略。法関係以外では、スポーツなどで 'vs.' と略されて使用されることが多い。

54. jury   [dʒú(ə)ri] [n] 陪審

Attorneys agreed on a **jury** of seven women and five men.
弁護士たちは、7人の女性と5人の男性で構成される陪審団に同意した。
UP swear in a jury　陪審員に所定の宣誓をさせる

55. civil   [sív(ə)l] [adj] 民事の

The firm's practice areas include **civil** litigation and federal employment law.
その会社の実務範囲には、民事訴訟と連邦雇用法が含まれる。
UP civil rights/union　公民権／民事団体

56. prison   [prízn] [n] 刑務所

The **prison** population rose 66 percent between 1995 and 2009.
刑務所人口は、1995年から2009年の間に66パーセント増加した。
UP sent/sentenced to prison　禁固刑を受ける

57. victim   [víktɪm] [n] 被害者

Once one **victim** comes forward, others will follow.
1人でも被害者が名乗り出れば、他の人もそれに続くだろう。
UP innocent/unsuspecting victim　無実の被害者

58. complaint   [kəmpléɪnt] [n] 告訴状, 告訴

The judge is acting on a **complaint** filed in June.
その裁判官は、6月に提起された告訴状に対して裁決している。
UP file/lodge a complaint　告訴する

59. military   [mílətèri | -təri, -tri] [adj] 軍の

The U.S. plans to put him on trial before a **military** jury.
米国は、軍の陪審の前に彼を審理するつもりだ。
UP military officer/personnel　軍の職員

60. county   [káʊnti] [n] 郡

He was elected to the **county** court in 1998 and assigned to the Supreme Court in 2006.
彼は1998年に郡裁判官に選ばれ、2006年には最高裁判官に任命された。
UP county office　郡事務所

Vocabulary for Law

Vocabulary Notes

_____
_____
_____
_____
_____
_____
_____
_____

To remember spelling, write new words many times.

Unit 2 Test Yourself

Quiz 1: Match the words and phrases with their meanings.

1. area _____   a. 軍の
2. evidence _____   b. 過程
3. military _____   c. 分野
4. criminal _____   d. 刑事上の
5. process _____   e. 被害者
6. victim _____   f. 資金
7. fund _____   g. 証拠

Quiz 2: Fill in the blanks with the best word from this unit.

| prison | alleged | damages | lawsuit | involved | financial | arrested |

1. For taxes, the company's _____ documents will be examined.
2. We're not sure if he really committed the crime, but it is _____ that he did.
3. She spent three years in _____ before being released.
4. I filed a _____ against my neighbors because their dog bit me.
5. My friend was _____ and taken away by the police.

Now check your answers on page 62.

Unit 2   17

Unit 3

61. decline [dɪkláɪn] [v] 拒否する

Police **declined** to release the names of the victims.
警察は，被害者の名前を公開することを拒否した。
UP decline a request/offer　要請を拒否する／申し出を拒否する

ポイント！ 下降するという意味もある。

62. dispute [dɪspjúːt] [v] 議論する

The view expressed in this article may be **disputed**.
この記事で述べられている見解は，物議を醸すことになるかもしれない。

[n] 紛争

Not all **disputes** need to be resolved in court.
すべての紛争が裁判で解決される必要があるわけではない。
UP border/labor dispute　境界紛争／労働紛争

63. hearing [hí(ə)rɪŋ] [n] 審理，聴聞

The attorney declined to comment after Friday's **hearing**.
その弁護士は，金曜日の審理の後にコメントすることを拒否した。
UP conduct/hold a hearing　聴聞会を開く

64. challenge [tʃælɪndʒ] [v] 異議を唱える

It is the first time these powers have been **challenged** at an open hearing.
これらの権力が公開審理で異議を唱えられたのは，これが初めてだ。

[n] 異議

He wondered if a **challenge** could be raised over the issue.
彼は，その問題について異議を唱えることができるのかどうか疑問に思った。
UP pose/present a challenge　異議を唱える

65. commission [kəmíʃən] [n] 委員会

Shim said the **commission** cannot comment on whether it will take action.
措置を講じるかどうかについて委員会がコメントすることはできないとシムは言った。
UP establish/set up a commission　委員会を立ち上げる

66. argument [áːrɡjʊmənt | áː-] [n] 弁論，主張

The **argument** for the defendants was based on clear evidence.
被告に対する弁論は，明確な証拠に基づいていた。
UP logical/balanced argument　論理的主張／偏りのない主張

67. create [kriéɪt, kríːeɪt] [v] 創設する

Last month, the governor **created** a commission to make recommendations on judges' salaries.
先月，知事は裁判官の給料に関する提案を行うための委員会を創設した。
UP create jobs/opportunities　仕事を創設する／機会を創設する

68. human rights   [hjúːmən] [ráɪts]   n   人権

They argued that the family's right to privacy falls under the **Human Rights** Act.
彼らは，家族のプライバシーの権利が人権法に該当すると主張した。
UP protect/violate human rights   人権を守る／人権を侵害する

69. bar   [báɚ | báː]   n   法廷，弁護士会

Only three percent passed the **bar** exam under the former system.
旧司法試験では，3％しか合格しなかった。
UP be admitted to the bar   弁護士として認可される

 bar exam で出ることが多い。その場合は司法試験。

70. conduct   [kəndʌ́kt]   v   行う

An important study on jury behaviour was **conducted** by Professor Thomas at University College London.
ロンドン大学のトーマス教授によって，陪審員の振る舞いに関する重要な研究が行われた。

[kǽndʌkt, -dəkt | kɔ́n-]   n   行為

The alleged **conduct** took place in the UK.
申し立てられた行為は，英国で起こった。
UP appropriate/professional conduct   適切な行為／専門的な行為

 名詞形と動詞形では，発音強勢が異なるため，注意が必要。名詞では，強勢は前で，動詞では後ろとなる。

71. panel   [pǽnl]   n   陪審，公開討論会

A three-judge appeals **panel** found that the claims were fair.
3人の上訴陪審員は，その主張を正当だと判断した。
UP convene/assemble a panel   陪審を召集する

72. economic   [èkənámɪk, iːk- | -nɔ́m-]   adj   経済上の

More than 300 lawsuits seek **economic** damages for businesses and individuals.
300件以上の訴訟で，企業と個人のための経済的損害賠償を求めている。
UP economic growth/development   経済成長／経済開発

73. settlement   [séṭlmənt]   n   和解

That doesn't include any of the money paid in **settlements** and judgments.
それは，和解や判決で支払われた金を一切含んでいない。
UP come to/reach a settlement   和解に至る

74. community   [kəmjúːnəṭi]   n   集団

Sheen will be required to abide by jail rules while out in the **community**.
社会復帰している間も，シーンは刑務所規則を守る必要がある。
UP business/scientific community   ビジネスの集団／科学の集団

Unit 3   19

75. suspect [səspékt] v 疑いをかける

His girlfriend is **suspected** of helping in the escape.
彼の恋人は，逃亡を助けた容疑をかけられた。

[sʌ́spekt] n 容疑者

The rulings will change the ways police, lawyers and criminal **suspects** interact.
その判決は，警察，弁護士，そして犯罪の容疑者が接触する方法を変えるだろう。
UP interrogate/question a suspect　容疑者を尋問する

76. employee [ɪmplɔ́ɪíː, em-, -plɔ́ɪiː] n 従業員

Judges received no pay increase, but 200,000 other state **employees** received raises.
裁判官は昇給しなかったが，他の20万人の国家公務員は昇給した。
UP hire/take on an employee　従業員を雇う

77. media [míːdiə] n マスコミ

The company confirmed **media** reports that it received the offer on July 28.
その会社は，7月28日に申し込みを受けたというマスコミの報道を確認した。
UP local/national media　地方のマスコミ／全国的なマスコミ

　単数形は medium。

78. rate [réɪt] n 率

The city always had a high crime **rate**: almost four times as many murders in 1981 as last year.
その都市は常に高い犯罪率があり，昨年は1981年の殺人件数のほぼ4倍だった。
UP birth/death/divorce rate　出生率／死亡率／離婚率

79. organization [ɔ̀ːrɡənɪzéɪʃən | ɔ̀ːɡənaɪz-] n 組織，機構

A report released by the human rights **organization** documents the criminal treatment.
人権団体が公表した報告書では，犯罪者の処遇について記録している。
UP establish/form an organization　組織を作る

　イギリス英語のスペルは，organisation となる。

80. accuse [əkjúːz] v 訴える

The government has **accused** international media organizations of focusing on negative news.
政府は，否定的なニュースを取り扱ったとして国際的なマスコミ組織を訴えた。
UP falsely accused　偽って訴えられる

accused [əkjúːzd] n 被告人，被疑者

Two of the **accused** were sentenced to death.
被告人の2人は死刑を宣告された。

　たいていの場合は "the" が前につく。

81. deny [dɪnáɪ] v 否定する

He **denied** trying to hide the criminal case from the Court.
彼は，刑事事件を法廷から隠そうとしたことを否定した。
UP strongly/vehemently deny　激しく否定する

20　*Vocabulary for Law*

82. investigation [ɪnvèstəgéɪʃən] [n] 捜査

The Justice Department's criminal **investigation** of the oil spill included a 40-lawyer environmental crimes team.
司法省の石油流出の犯罪捜査は，40人の環境犯罪弁護士団が関わった。
UP carry out/conduct an investigation　捜査を行う

83. grant [grænt | grɑ́:nt] [v] 認める，与える

The state's highest court **granted** the request for a direct appeal.
州の最高裁判所は，直接上訴の要求を認めた。
UP grant permission/immunity　許可を与える／法的免除を与える

84. award [əwɔ́ɚd | əwɔ́:d] [v] 与える，裁定する

In Verni v Lanzaro, a jury **awarded** $105 million in damages over a drunk driving crash.
ベルニ対ランザロの訴訟で，陪審員は飲酒運転事故に対して1億5百万ドルの損害賠償を裁定した。

[n] 賠償金，賞

The ruling included a damages **award** of $7.5 million.
判決には，750万ドルの損害賠償金が含まれた。
UP grant/confer an award　賞を与える

85. committee [kəmíti] [n] 委員，委員会

I have served on the banking **committee** for eight years.
私は，8年間銀行委員を務めた。
UP organize/set up a committee　委員会を組織する

86. executive [ɪgzékjʊṭɪv, eg-] [n] 重役

The firm named the former **executive** committee member as managing partner for Hong Kong.
その法律事務所は，元重役を香港の業務執行社員に指名した。
UP business/corporate executive　会社の重役

87. global [glóʊb(ə)l | glóʊ-] [adj] 世界的な

Jones Day is one of the **global** law firms doing business in São Paulo.
ジョーンズ・デイは，サンパウロにある世界的な法律事務所の1つです。
UP global economy/trade　世界経済／世界貿易

88. individual [ìndəvídʒuəl, -dʒʊl] [adj] 個々の

The tax office declined to comment due to a policy of not discussing **individual** cases.
税務署は，個々の事例を議論しないという方針によってコメントすることを拒否した。
UP individual rights/needs　個人的権利／個人的要求

89. article [ɑ́ɚṭɪkl | ɑ́:-] [n] 条文，条項

They are charged with sending funds to Iraq, contrary to **articles** 3(a) and 11(4) of the United Nations Sanctions Order.
彼らは国連制裁命令のうち3(a)条と11(4)条に違反し，イラクに資金を送ったとして告発された。
UP according to article　～の条文によると

90. benefit [bénəfɪt | -fɪt] [v] ためになる，助けになる

The donated books will greatly **benefit** the students of law in Kosovo.
寄付された本は，コソボの法学生の大いなる助けとなる。
UP benefit society/the community　社会のためになる／共同体のためになる

Unit 3

Vocabulary Notes

_____
_____
_____
_____
_____
_____
_____
_____

Write new words in the *Vocabulary Notebook* on Page 58.

 Unit 3 Test Yourself

Quiz 1: Match the words and phrases with their meanings.

1. investigation _____   a. 認める
2. bar _____   b. 捜査
3. deny _____   c. 行う
4. human rights _____   d. 異議を唱える
5. challenge _____   e. 法廷
6. conduct _____   f. 否定する
7. grant _____   g. 人権

Quiz 2: Fill in the blanks with the best word from this unit.

accused   economic   article   executive   settlement   rate   award

1. He was _____ of murder, but later released.

2. It was an _____ decision that affected everyone working at the organization.

3. The interest _____ is very high right now. It's not a good time to buy a house.

4. People are not spending much money because they are worried about the global _____ situation.

5. My boss and I reached a _____, so we didn't have to take the case to court.

Now check your answers on page 62.

Unit 4

91. ban [bǽn] v 禁止する

Cell phone use is **banned** only when you're driving.
運転中のみ，携帯電話の使用は禁止されている。

n 禁止

Defense lawyers argued at trial that the **ban** was necessary to safeguard the traditional understanding of marriage.
被告側弁護団は，結婚に対する伝統的な理解を守るために，禁止は必要であると裁判で主張した。
UP impose/place/put a ban on ～を禁止する

92. patent [pǽtnt | péɪt-, pǽt-] n 特許

Nokia and Apple have both unleashed **patent** suits against rivals in the smartphone market.
ノキアとアップルの両社は，スマートフォン市場のライバルに特許訴訟を起こした。
UP obtain/hold a patent 特許を得る

93. site [sáɪt] n サイト（インターネットのサイト）

The search page of Google's Hong Kong **site** was accessible from the mainland on Tuesday.
グーグルの香港サイトの検索ページは，火曜日に本土からアクセスできた。

n 場所，敷地

The building was just a few hundred metres from the former **site** of the prison.
その建物は前刑務所のあった場所から，たった数百メートルの所にあった。
UP construction/camping site 建設現場／キャンプ場

> **ポイント！** この単語は，website が短くなったもの。

94. reject [rɪdʒékt] v はねつける，認めない

Grimm **rejected** the defendants' claim that the deleted files were actually saved elsewhere.
グリムは，削除されたファイルが実はどこか別の場所で保存されていたという被告の主張をはねつけた。
UP reject completely/outright 完全にはねつける

95. council [káʊnsl] n 審議会，議会，委員会

The **council** narrowly rejected the ban in 2008.
審議会は，2008年にその禁止令をかろうじて否認した。
UP student council 学生委員会・学生自治会

> **ポイント！** city council は，アメリカでは市議会を意味し，イギリスでは local council という。

96. contract [kántrækt | kɔ́n-] n 契約

The automaker says the **contract** allows it to hire new workers at $14 per hour.
自動車メーカーは，その契約で新しい労働者を雇うために時給14ドルを支払うと述べた。
UP sign/enter into a contract 契約を結ぶ

97. economy [ɪkánəmi | ɪkɔ́n-] n 経済

Check! 72. The government reported that the **economy** slowed significantly in April.
政府は，4月に経済が著しく低迷したと発表した。
UP capitalist/free-market economy 資本主義経済／自由市場経済

23

98. amendment [əmén(d)mənt] n （法令の）修正（案）

The lawsuit was filed by a voter opposed to the **amendment**.
その法令の修正案に反対する有権者によって訴訟が起こされた。
UP propose/ratify an amendment　修正を提案する／修正を認可する

 特にアメリカ憲法の追加や修正に関して使用される。

99. guilty [gílti] adj 罪を犯した，有罪の

If found **guilty**, they would face prison terms of up to 10 years.
もし有罪ならば，彼らは懲役10年以下の刑になるだろう。
UP plead guilty　有罪を認める

100. board [bɔ́əd | bɔ́ːd] n 委員会，役員

It's essential to consult with other **board** members before acting.
行動を起こす前に他の委員と相談することは，必要不可欠だ。
UP parole board　仮釈放委員会

101. statute [stǽtʃuːt] n 法令，法規，制定法

The challenged **statute** imposes sentences of up to 15 years in prison.
異議を申し立てられた法令では，15年以内の懲役刑を科す。
UP statute of limitations　出訴期限法

102. major [méɪdʒɚ | -dʒə] adj 主要な

After three days of flying bans, all **major** airlines claimed that authorities had been overly cautious.
3日間の飛行禁止令の後，全ての主要な航空会社は当局が過度に慎重だったと主張した。
UP major problem/concern　主要な問題

103. fraud [frɔ́ːd] n 詐欺

He was put in prison on six counts of **fraud**.
彼は6つの詐欺行為で，刑務所に入れられた。
UP commit/perpetrate fraud　詐欺を犯す

104. role [róʊl | rə́ʊl] n 任務，役

Hughes left his position to take a non-legal **role** in the bank's front office.
ヒューズは，銀行の本部で法律に関しない任務に就くために今の職を退いた。
UP assume/take on a role　任務を引き受ける

105. serve [sə́ːv | sə́ːv] v 服役する

Amos is **serving** 121 months in federal prison.
エーモスは連邦刑務所に121ヵ月間服役している。

v 務める

He most recently **served** as an assistant U.S. attorney.
彼はごく最近，アメリカの弁護助手として務めた。
UP serve on a jury　陪審を務める

Vocabulary for Law

106. Inc. [ɪŋk] [adj] 会社

Google **Inc.** and Verizon Communications **Inc.** are close to finalizing a deal.
グーグルとベリゾンコミュニケーションズは，もう間もなく契約を交わす。

社名の後に用いる。Incorporated の略。

107. target [tɑ́ɚgɪt | tɑ́ː-] [n] 標的，対象

Even if evidence cannot be challenged, the person who collected it may be an easy **target** for opposing counsel.
たとえ証拠に異議を唱えられなかったとしても，証拠を集めた人が相手の弁護人には容易な標的になるかもしれない。

UP target audience/area　対象の聴衆／対象の場所

108. aid [éɪd] [v] 援助する，助ける

He and other human rights lawyers and academics **aided** villagers in protecting their rights.
彼や他の人権専門の弁護士や大学教員らは，村人たちの権利を守る手助けをした。

[n] 援助

The U.K. pays far more than most other countries for legal **aid**.
イギリスは法律扶助に他の国よりはるかに多くのお金を支払う。

UP extend/offer aid　援助を申し出る

109. judicial [dʒuːdíʃəl] [adj] 司法の

Stefanik was sentenced to 21 months in prison for threatening **judicial** employees in Boston.
ステファニックは，ボストンにおいて司法職員を脅迫したことで懲役21ヵ月の判決を下された。

UP judicial system/process　司法システム／司法過程

110. focus [fóʊkəs | fɔ́ʊ-] [v] 集中する

Focus on ways to contribute to your clients' success.
あなたの依頼人の成功に貢献するための方法に集中しなさい。

[n] 焦点

He started his career with General Motors, and has made automotive law a **focus** throughout his career.
彼はゼネラルモーターズでキャリアを始め，そして彼は生涯，自動車関連法律に焦点をあてた。

UP primary/main focus　主要な点

111. announce [ənáʊns] [v] 公表する

Judge Walker **announced** late Wednesday that he would issue his decision by noon.
ウォーカー裁判官は水曜日遅くに，彼の判決を正午までに下すと公表した。

UP announce one's resignation/retirement　退職を公表する

112. associate [əsóʊʃièɪt, -si- | əsóʊ-] [n] 社員，若手弁護士，インターン，準会員

The firm typically hired about 95 summer **associates** for its New York office.
その法律事務所は例によって，いつものようにニューヨークの事務所で約95人の夏期のインターンを雇った。

この単語は使い方により様々な意味になり，business associate として使用されると仕事を通した関係の人のことを指す。associate professor は，准教授を指す。法律では，associate は partner（check 11!）より下のレベルを表し，会社の所有権を持たない弁護士を意味する。例文にある summer associates といえば，法律を学ぶ学生のインターン生たちを意味する。

113. access　　　　　　　　　　[ǽkses]　[n]　利用の権利，アクセス，入手方法，接近

While the ruling would leave the plaintiffs with no **access** to the courts, they would not be without options.
その判決は，原告に裁判を受ける権利を認めないが，彼らは他の選択肢がないわけではなかった。

UP gain/get access to　〜に接近（出入り，面会）する

[v]　アクセスする，接近する

This action highlights the many risks employers face in **accessing** and using information obtained from online sites.
この行動は，社員がインターネットサイトでアクセスし，得た情報を使用する際に直面する多くのリスクを強調している。

114. spokesman　　　　　　　　[spóʊksmən | spóʊks-]　[n]　スポークスマン（広報係）

While not commenting on the Miami suit directly, a **spokesman** for Coca-Cola issued a comment by e-mail Thursday.
直接的なマイアミ訴訟についてのコメントではないが，コカ・コーラの広報は，木曜日に電子メールでコメントを出した。

ポイント！　同じ意味で，spokeswoman や spokesperson も使用される。

115. senior　　　　　　　　　　[síːnjɚ | -njə]　[adj]　上役の

"There is a need across the globe for the investigation of fraud," the former **senior** partner said.
「世界全体で詐欺行為の調査の必要がある」と，元上役のパートナーが言った。

UP senior adviser　上役の顧問

116. abuse　　　　　　　　　　[əbjúːs]　[n]　虐待

An investigation report identified six cases of alleged **abuse** by monks and teachers at the school.
調査報告では，学校での僧や教師による虐待とみられる6つのケースがあることが特定された。

UP emotional/physical abuse　感情的虐待／身体的虐待

117. sue　　　　　　　　　　　[súː | s(j)úː]　[v]　訴える

In Manhattan federal court he is now **suing** the police for $400,000.
マンハッタン連邦裁判所において，彼は現在，40万ドルの支払いを求めて警察を訴えている。

UP sue for damages　損害賠償で訴える

118. identify　　　　　　　　　[aɪdéntəfàɪ]　[v]　突きとめる，同一視する

The case team wanted to quickly **identify** documents that would help senior attorneys prepare for the case.
その訴訟チームは，上席の弁護士の訴訟準備を手伝うため，書類をすぐに突き止めたかった。

UP positively identify　確信を持って突き止める

119. determine　　　　　　　　[dɪtɚ́ːmɪn | -tɚ́ː-]　[v]　決心する，決断する

Jury questioning will help **determine** how much they know and what they think about the charges.
陪審質問は，その告発に関して彼らがどのくらい知っていて，どのように思っているかを決定する助けになる。

120. property　　　　　　　　　[prɑ́pəɾi | prɔ́pə-]　[n]　財産

That has led to some patent lawsuits that claim **property** rights over large areas of the Internet.
それはインターネットの広範囲なエリアにおいての財産権を請求するいくつかの特許訴訟を引き起こした。

[n]　所有地

The family was living in the **property** at the time and did not break the rules.
その家族は当時その所有地に住んでいた。そして，彼らはルールを破らなかった。

UP private/public property　私的所有地／公共の所有地

Vocabulary for Law

Vocabulary Notes

_____
_____
_____
_____
_____
_____
_____
_____

Try using new words in a sentence.

Unit 4 Test Yourself

Quiz 1: Match the words and phrases with their meanings.

1. access   _____   a. 決心する
2. associate   _____   b. 詐欺
3. fraud   _____   c. 接近する
4. determine   _____   d. 法令
5. property   _____   e. 財産
6. patent   _____   f. 特許
7. statute   _____   g. 社員

Quiz 2: Fill in the blanks with the best word from this unit.

| banned | contract | aid | Inc. | council | sue | accessed |

1. There is a big debate about whether African countries should receive _____ from the U.S.

2. If you don't pay the money you owe me, I'll _____ you!

3. I'm very proud to have been elected to the city _____ .

4. You will have to sign a _____ with the company when you start your new job.

5. Tobacco is strictly _____ on campus.

Now check your answers on page 62.

Unit 4   27

Unit 5

121. expert [ékspə:t | -pə:t] [n] 専門家
"They think these people can help them," said a family law **expert** in Nashville.
「彼らはこれらの人々が自分たちを助けてくれると考えている」と，ナッシュビルで家族法の専門家は言った。
UP call in/consult an expert 専門家を呼ぶ／専門家に相談する

122. administration [ədmìnəstréɪʃən] [n] 運営，経営陣
Your managing partner or director of **administration** should review these reports.
あなたの経営パートナーまたは運営の管理者は，これらの報告を再検討すべきだ。
UP university/hospital administration 大学運営／病院運営

[n] 政権，政府
The Obama **administration** was surprised to learn that Kennedy's final opinion was different from the original.
オバマ政権は，ケネディの最後の意見がオリジナルのものと異なることを知り驚いた。

123. court of appeals [kɔ́ət | kɔ́:t][əpí:lz] [n] 高等裁判所

In January, the **court of appeals** granted Rosenthal a new trial for what he claims the firm owes him.
1月に高等裁判所は，ローゼンサルがその会社は彼に支払いの義務があるとする主張に対しての新たな裁判を始めることを認めた。

124. witness [wítnəs] [v] 目撃する
There were 25 to 30 other people around who **witnessed** the shooting.
銃撃を目撃した人が周りに，25から30人いた。

[n] 証拠
We included as much evidence as we could from expert **witnesses**.
我々は私たちが鑑定人から集めることができたのと同じくらい，証拠を集めることが出来た。
UP expert witness 鑑定人

125. conflict [kánflɪkt | kɔ́n-] [n] 闘争
In Texas, the group has taken actions that are in **conflict** with the land-use laws.
テキサスでは，そのグループが土地利用法に矛盾していることに対して行動を取った。
UP religious/ethnic conflict 宗教闘争／民族闘争

126. judgment [dʒʌ́dʒmənt] [n] 判決
Check! 109.
The Supreme Court delivered a **judgment** concerning restrictions on the flow of fuel and electricity to Gaza.
最高裁判所がガザへの燃料や電気の流れを制限する判決を下した。
UP hand down a judgment 判決を言い渡す

ポイント！ イギリス英語でのつづりは judgement。

127. allegation [æ̀lɪɡéɪʃən] [n] 主張，陳述，申し立て

Without direct evidence, I would not be willing to make a direct **allegation**.
直接的な証拠なしに，私は直接的な陳述をすることを望まないだろう。
UP deny/reject an allegation 主張を否定する／主張を退ける

28

128. response　　　　　　　[rɪspáns | -spɔ́ns]　[n]　返答

In the written **response**, the department took responsibility for the error.
文書による回答によれば，その省は失敗の責任を負った。
UP give/make a response　返答する

129. arm　　　　　　　　　[áɚm | ɑ́:m]　[v]　武装させる

Tens of thousands of **armed** police patrolled the deserted streets of Kashmir.
何万もの武装した警官は，人通りのないカシミールの通りをパトロールした。

　　　　　　　　　　　　　　　　　　　　　　[n]　武器

The suspected Russian **arms** dealer is tired of prison life.
容疑をかけられているロシアの武器商人は，投獄生活にうんざりしている。
UP armed conflict　武力衝突

130. commit　　　　　　　[kəmít]　[v]　〜を犯す

He is subject to fines and must give up all vehicles and property used to **commit** the crime.
彼は，罰金を科せられ，その罪を犯す際に使用した全ての乗り物や財産をあきらめなければならない。
UP commit murder/perjury　殺人を犯す／偽証を犯す

131. despite　　　　　　　[dɪspáɪt]　[prep]　〜にもかかわらず

Despite losing the decision, Carter said, "I believe the judge did what he thought was right."
判決で負けたにもかかわらず，「裁判官が正しいと思った判決を下したと信じる」とカーターは述べた。

132. congress　　　　　　 [káŋgrəs | kɔ́ŋgres]　[n]　議会

Congress approved the special agreement more quickly than he had anticipated.
議会が彼が予測していたよりも早く特別な協定に賛成した。
UP convene/hold a congress　議会を召集する／議会を開く

> **ポイント!**　たいてい大文字で使用される。

133. corporate　　　　　　[kɔ́ɚp(ə)rət | kɔ́:-]　[adj]　企業の，法人組織の

Corporate lawyers have moved from large team-based practices to providing counsel in connection with day-to-day business.
企業の弁護士は，大きなチーム形式での業務体系から，その日その日の業務に関連して助言を与える体系に移行した。
UP corporate sponsor　企業のスポンサー

Check! 106.

134. prosecution　　　　　[pràsɪkjú:ʃən | prɔ̀s-]　[n]　検察，起訴

He couldn't argue that he hadn't received a fair trial because of the way the **prosecution** acted.
彼は検察の動きにより，正当な裁判を受けられなかったと主張出来なかった。
UP face prosecution　起訴に直面する

Check! 43.

Unit 5　29

135. convict　　　[kənvíkt]　[v]　有罪を宣告する
The men were **convicted** after a six-week trial at the court.
その男性たちは，裁判所で6週間裁判を行った後に有罪を宣告された。
UP convicted to ... years　～年の有罪を宣告された

　　　　　　　　　　　　　[kάnvɪkt]　[n]　罪人
Gunshots were exchanged but the **convict** was arrested without anyone being injured.
銃弾が飛び交ったが，けが人はなく，その罪人は逮捕された。

136. project　　　[prάdʒekt, -dʒɪkt | prɔ́dʒ-]　[n]　事業
Not every government **project** must have an impact on every congressional district.
全ての政府事業が全ての下院議員選挙区に影響を及ぼさなければならないとは限らない。
UP carry out/do a project　事業を行う

137. threat　　　[θrét]　[n]　脅威
As foreign secretary, he promoted Iran as the next "**threat**."
外務大臣として，彼はイランを次の「脅威」と位置づけた。
UP issue/make a threat　脅す

138. establish　　　[ɪstǽblɪʃ, es-]　[v]　確立する
The goal has been to **establish** a collective response to threats from al-Qaida.
目標はアルカイダからの脅威に集団的返答を確立することだ。
UP establish a relationship/system　関係を確立する／システムを確立する

139. technology　　　[teknάlədʒi | -nɔ́l-]　[n]　科学技術
Advances in **technology**, while aiding the corporate world and the consumer, also aid the criminal.
科学技術の進歩は，実業界や消費者を手助けする一方で，犯罪者もまた助けることになる。
UP computer/information technology　コンピュータ技術／情報技術

140. count　　　[káʊnt]　[n]　訴因
Blagojevich faces up to four hundred years in prison and $6 million in fines, if convicted on all **counts**.
もし全ての訴因で有罪を宣告されるなら，ブラゴヤビッチは400年以下の服役と600万ドルの罰金に直面することになるだろう。
UP guilty on all counts　全ての訴因で有罪

141. stay　　　[stéɪ]　[n]　停止，凍結
Lawyers asked the court to lift the **stay** just a few hours after the administration announced its new position.
弁護士たちは，経営陣が新しい職を公表したわずか数時間後に，その停止を解くよう裁判所に頼んだ。
UP issue/grant a stay　凍結する

142. motion　　　[móʊʃən | móʊ-]　[n]　申請
Prosecutors had filed a **motion** asking that his five-year sentence be increased.
検察官たちは，彼の5年の判決が増えるように求める申請をした。
UP grant/deny a motion　申請を認める／申請を認めない

143. investor [ɪnvéstɚ | -tə] n 投資者

An **investor** who lost $1 million, for example, wouldn't want to spend $200,000 to $300,000 in court.
例えば，100万ドルを失った投資者は，裁判所に20万から30万ドルの費用を支払いたいとは思わないだろう。
UP institutional/private investor　機関投資家／個人投資家

144. medical [médɪk(ə)l] adj 医学的な

The plaintiff will need to have some **medical** evidence supporting the claim.
原告は主張を裏付ける医学的証拠を必要とするだろう。
UP medical center/school　医学センター／医学部（医科大学）

145. majority [mədʒɔ́:rəti | -dʒɔ́r-] n 大多数，多数派

Check! 102.
Hebert said he prefers the current makeup of the board — with a **majority** of lawyers and a minority of public members.
ハバートは，大多数の弁護士と少数の市民で構成された現在の委員会を好むと言った。
UP clear/overwhelming majority　明白な大多数／圧倒的大多数

146. region [rí:dʒən] n 地域

There have always been regional differences, but the differences from **region** to **region** may be becoming more pronounced.
常に地域格差はあったが，地域と地域の違いはより明白になっているかもしれない。
UP border/remote region　国境の地域／遠方の地域

147. respond [rɪspánd | -spɔ́nd] v 答える，返答する

Check! 128.
He filed lawsuits, but often failed to **respond** to motions, meet deadlines or appear in court.
彼は訴訟を起こしたが，しかし，しばしば申し立てに返答しなかったり，締め切りを守らなかったり，もしくは，裁判所に出廷しなかった。
UP respond clearly/vaguely　はっきりと答える／あいまいに答える

148. violate [váɪəlèɪt] v 違反する

The suit claimed the gas supplier **violated** state and federal fair trade laws.
その訴訟は，ガス供給者が州および国の公正取引法に違反したと主張した。
UP violate a rule/an agreement　規則に違反する／合意に違反する

149. finding [fáɪndɪŋ] n 調査結果

The **findings**, based on responses from 1,873 partners, provide information about the firms.
1,873人のパートナーからの回答に基づいた調査結果は，その会社についての情報を提供する。
UP preliminary findings　予備調査結果

> **ポイント！** 多くの場合，複数形で使用される。

150. injury [índʒ(ə)ri] n 負傷

The nurse would not release any information about the woman's **injuries**.
看護師は，その女性の怪我に関する情報を公表しようとしなかった。
UP suffer/sustain an injury　怪我に苦しむ／怪我を負う

Unit 5

Vocabulary Notes

Review new words often.

Unit 5 Test Yourself

Quiz 1: Match the words and phrases with their meanings.

1. stay _____   a. 答える
2. threat _____   b. 違反する
3. prosecution _____ c. 判決
4. judgment _____   d. 検察
5. violate _____   e. 脅威
6. respond _____   f. 停止
7. injury _____   g. 負傷

Quiz 2: Fill in the blanks with the best word from this unit.

| expert | convict | findings | arms | despite | projects | regions |

1. The Alps is one of the most beautiful _____ in Europe.
2. Many people worked hard to complete these _____ on time.
3. He became a law _____ by studying it for many years.
4. In many countries it is illegal to carry _____ outside of the military.
5. _____ studying hard, I didn't get a good mark on the test.

Now check your answers on page 62.

32 Vocabulary for Law

Unit 6

151. approach　　　　　[əpróʊtʃ | əpróʊtʃ]　[v]　交渉する，近づく
Twenty-five relatives of the crash victims have **approached** my legal firm.
その墜落事故被害者の25人の親類が，私の法律事務所と交渉した。

152. conference　　　　[kɑ́nf(ə)rəns | kɔ́n-]　[n]　会議
The partners spoke at the annual legal **conference**.
パートナーたちは，年次弁護士会議で話した。
UP press/news conference　記者会見

153. dismiss　　　　　　[dɪsmís]　[v]　棄却する，退ける
The judge **dismissed** an additional charge of fraud.
その裁判官は，追加の不正行為の訴えを棄却した。
　　　　　　　　　　　　　　　　　　　　　　　　　　　[v]　解雇する
He has filed a case claiming that he was unfairly **dismissed**.
彼は，不当に解雇されたと主張する裁判を起こした。
UP dismiss out of hand　即座に退ける

154. investigate　　　　[ɪnvéstəgèɪt]　[v]　調査する

The coast guard said it was **investigating** whether the fishing boat entered the exclusive economic zone.
沿岸警備隊は，その漁船が排他的経済水域に入ったかどうかを調査していると言った。
UP thoroughly/fully investigate　徹底的に調査する

155. section　　　　　　[sékʃən]　[n]　節，項
Section 613 of the law will enable national or state banks to open branches in other states.
その法律の613項によると，国立銀行や州立銀行の支店を他の州に置くことは可能である。
UP according to Section　〜項によると

> ポイント！　ここの section は，一般的に使用する「部分」や「区画」という意味とは異なる。

156. senate　　　　　　[sénət]　[n]　上院
The **Senate** passed both the $26 billion jobs bill and the border security bill.
上院は260億ドルの雇用促進法案および国境警備法案の両方を可決した。
UP convene/dissolve the senate　上院を召集する／上院を解散する

> ポイント！　通常は大文字。

157. enforcement　　　[ɪnfɔ́ːrsmənt, en- | -fɔ́ːsmənt]　[n]　施行
The law is designed to allow **enforcement** officers to prosecute offenders before terrorist attacks can be carried out.
その法律は，テロ攻撃が遂行される前に，施行係が犯罪者を訴追できることを定めている。
UP rigid/strict enforcement　厳正な施行

> ポイント！　law enforcement では，犯罪者を捕まえるために関わっている警察などを表す。

33

158. regulation [règjʊléɪʃən] n 規定，法規

Regulation (3) requires that the defence be given adequate time to respond.
規定(3)は，被告側が答えるのに十分な時間を与えられることを義務付けている。

n 規制

The **regulation** of medical practice is a state and not a federal responsibility.
医療業務の規制は，連邦ではなく州の責任である。
UP adopt/enact a regulation　規定を採用する／規定を制定する

159. immigration [ìməgréɪʃən] n 移住，入植

The 82-year-old is accused of lying during **immigration** hearings in 2005 and 2006.
その82歳の人は2005年と2006年の移住審理の際に嘘をついたと訴えられている。
UP immigration law/policy　移民法／移民政策

160. juror [dʒʊ́(ə)rɚ | -rə] n 陪審員

Check! 54.

The Justice said that the **juror** had not understood the trial judge's instructions to the jury.
その判事は，陪審員がその審理裁判官の陪審への指示を理解していなかっただろうと言った。
UP potential/prospective juror　潜在的陪審員

161. potential [pəténʃəl] adj 潜在的な，可能性がある

Two years ago, 600 **potential** jurors were dismissed after one revealed he had done some internet research.
2年前，1人の男性があるインターネット調査を行ったことを明らかにした後，600人の潜在陪審員が解雇された。
UP potential problem/conflict　潜在的な問題／潜在的な争い

162. liability [làɪəbíləṭi] n 責任

She continued the product **liability** suit she had filed against the drug company.
彼女は，その製薬会社に対して起こした製造物責任訴訟を継続した。
UP accept/assume liability　責任を負う

163. divorce [dɪvɔ́ɚs | -vɔ́ːs] n 離婚

When Kenneth filed for **divorce**, he asked the court to enforce his and Cheryl's agreement.
ケネスが離婚の申請をした時，彼は裁判での彼とシェリルの契約の施行を頼んだ。
UP file/sue for divorce　離婚の申し立て（訴え）をする

164. jail [dʒéɪl] n 刑務所

He faced a sentence of up to seven years in **jail**.
彼は，懲役7年の刑に直面した。
UP go/be sent to jail　刑務所へ行く／刑務所に送られる

165. illegal [ì(l)líːɡ(ə)l] adj 不法な

Check! 6.

We should improve the use of technology to prevent **illegal** immigration.
私たちは，不法移民を防ぐための技術の利用を改善すべきだ。
UP illegal alien　不法な外国人

> **ポイント！** legal の反対で，"unlegal" とは言わない。"L" で始まる単語は，"il" を付けることで反対の意味になることが多い。

Vocabulary for Law

166. decade [dékeɪd] n 10年間

A complex international legal battle has lasted more than a **decade** about arresting the former President.
前大統領の逮捕についての複雑な国際的法廷闘争は，10年以上続いた。
UP past/previous decade 過去10年間

167. consumer [kənsú:mɚ | -s(j)ú:mə] n 消費者

The plaintiffs also claim that there are violations of California **consumer** laws.
原告はさらに，カリフォルニア消費者法の違反があると主張する。
UP consumer protection 消費者保護

168. cite [sáɪt] v 法廷に召喚する

A company in Louisiana was **cited** in May for polluting nearby waters.
ルイジアナ州のある会社は5月に，近隣の水域汚染に関して法廷に召喚された。

v 引用する

See the *Boston Globe* story I **cited** earlier for an overview of the case.
その訴訟の概観のために，私が以前引用したボストン・グローブの記事を参照して下さい。
UP cite evidence/an example 証拠を引用する／例を引用する

169. brief [brí:f] adj 簡潔な

Nine members of Congress made **brief** remarks to the conference.
9人の国会議員が，会議への簡潔な意見を述べた。

n 令状，意見書

The **brief** was filed in a court in Arizona on the same day as the deadline for such filings.
その令状は，アリゾナの裁判所において，そのような提出物の締切日と同日に提出された。
UP draw up/file a brief 令状を作成する

 amicus brief という法廷助言者による意見書のような具体的なものもある。

170. minister [mínɪstɚ | -tə] n 大臣，長官

Germany's justice **minister** says she is considering changes to income tax laws.
ドイツの法務大臣は，所得税法の変更を考えていると述べた。
UP foreign/interior/prime minister 外務大臣／内務大臣／首相

 アメリカでは secretary を使う。

171. material [mətí(ə)riəl] adj 重要な

The law prevents a doctor from being sued for not providing what might be **material** information to her patient.
その法律は，患者にとって重要な情報かもしれないことを提示しなかったことに対して，医者が訴えられるのを防ぐ。

n 資料

Such **material** is already banned from publication on Australian websites.
そのような資料は，オーストラリアのウェブサイト上の出版物からすでに禁止されている。
UP raw material 原料

Unit 6 35

172. block [blák | blɔ́k] v 防ぐ

The filters can **block** searches from inside China and block access to individual pages appearing within the search.
そのフィルターは中国国内からの検索，および検索の中で見つかった個々のページへのアクセスを防ぐことができる。
UP **block out/off** さえぎる／ふさぐ

173. provision [prəvíʒən] n 条項，但し書き

A major development is the inclusion of a **provision** criminalizing the transport of dangerous or radioactive materials.
大きな進歩は，危険物あるいは放射性物質の輸送を法で処罰する条項を含んだことである。
UP **violate a provision** 条項に違反する

174. obtain [əbtéɪn] v 得る

The first thing the attorney must do is **obtain** the evidence.
弁護士が最初にしなければならないことは，証拠を得ることである。
UP **obtain permission/a license** 許可を得る／ライセンスを得る

175. treaty [tríːti] n 条約

The Armenian-Turkish border was defined by the **Treaty** of Kars on October 13, 1921.
アルメニアとトルコの国境は1921年10月13日にカルスの条約によって定義された。
UP **work out/negotiate a treaty** 条約を取り決める

176. citizen [sítəzn | -sn, -zn] n 国民

The plaintiffs were Nigerian **citizens** who claimed that British and Nigerian companies had violated human rights.
原告は，イギリス，そしてナイジェリアの会社が人権を侵害したと主張したナイジェリアの国民たちだった。
UP **upright/upstanding citizen** 高潔な国民

177. vehicle [víː(h)ɪkl | víːəkl | víːɪkl] n 乗物

A radar gun is used to determine a **vehicle**'s exact speed.
速度測定装置は，乗物の正確な速度を測定するために使用される。
UP **drive/operate a vehicle** 乗り物を操縦する

178. secretary [sékrətèri | -tri, -təri] n 長官，大臣

The Justice **Secretary** has announced plans to close 157 courts to save £15.3 million a year.
法務長官は，年間1,530万ポンド削減のため157の裁判所を閉鎖する計画を発表した。
UP **secretary of state** 国務長官

イギリスでは minister を使う。

179. campaign [kæmpéɪn] n 選挙運動，選挙戦

The **campaign** has been nasty and has not focused on policy issues.
その選挙運動はたちが悪く，政策問題に焦点をあてていない。
UP **launch/mount a campaign** 選挙運動を始める

180. affect [əfékt] v ～に影響を及ぼす

Obama will have a number of very difficult decisions to make that will **affect** us all.
オバマは，私たちすべてに影響を及ぼす，数多くのとても難しい結論を下さなければならない。
UP **affect deeply/strongly** 深刻に影響を及ぼす

Vocabulary Notes

_____
_____
_____
_____
_____
_____
_____
_____
_____

Try using new words in your daily life.

Unit 6 Test Yourself

Quiz 1: Match the words and phrases with their meanings.

1. enforcement _____
2. provision _____
3. dismiss _____
4. material _____
5. affect _____
6. brief _____
7. cite _____

a. 施行
b. 令状
c. 条項
d. 引用する
e. 〜に影響を及ぼす
f. 重要な
g. 棄却する

Quiz 2: Fill in the blanks with the best word from this unit.

| investigating | jail | citizen | obtain | treaty | consumer | juror |

1. The two countries finally signed a peace _____.
2. After the police caught him, he was put in _____ for three years.
3. You have to take an eye test before you can _____ a driver's license.
4. Are you an American _____?
5. The police are _____ the crime scene right now.

Now check your answers on page 62.

Unit 6   37

Unit 7

181. impact [ímpækt] [n] 影響, 衝撃
He pointed out that mistakes in case rulings can have global **impact**.
彼は，裁決の誤りは世界的な影響があることを指摘した。
UP have/make an impact on　〜に影響を与える

182. schedule [skédʒuːl, -dʒʊl | ʃédjuːl] [v] 予定する
A hearing on the motion is **scheduled** for Sept. 1.
その動議に関する聴取は，9月1日に予定されている。

[n] 別表, 予定

Schedule 3 of the 2004 act contains lists of countries that are safe for the purposes of the refugee convention.
2004年の制定法の別表3は，難民総会開催に際して可能な国々のリストを含んでいる。
UP plan/prepare/draw up a schedule　予定を立てる

183. ensure [ɪnʃʊər, en- | -ʃɔː, -ʃʊə] [v] 保証する
We want to **ensure** training is available to every judge who wants it.
私たちは，訓練を望む裁判官なら誰でも利用可能であるということを保証したい。
UP ensure safety/success　安全を保証する／成功を保証する

184. defend [dɪfénd] [v] 弁護する
Check! 51.
These allegations are not true, and we plan to **defend** against them.
これらの申し立ては真実ではない。よって，私たちは彼らを弁護する計画である。
UP defend the action/decision　行動を弁護する／決定を弁護する

185. estimate [éstəmèit] [v] 判断する, 見積もる
The judge **estimated** that the trial should be complete by July 22.
裁判官は，その裁判が7月22日までに終了するだろうと判断した。

[éstəmət] [n] 見積もり

Estimates of the cost of investigating the company range between $35 to $50 million.
その会社の調査にかかる費用の見積もりは，3,500万ドルから5,000万ドルにわたる。
UP ballpark/rough estimate　おおよその見積もり

186. constitutional [kànstət(j)úːʃ(ə)nəl | kɔ̀nstɪtjúː-] [adj] 憲法上の
Many **constitutional** issues come down to the single question of whether or not Congress has the power to regulate.
多くの憲法上の問題はすべて，議会が規制するための力があるかどうかという1つの疑問にかかっている。
UP constitutional right/amendment　憲法上の権利／憲法上の改正

187. revenue [révən(j)ùː | -njùː] [n] 収入
Revenue per lawyer at the Washington firm rose by 3.6 percent last year.
ワシントンの法律事務所の弁護士1人あたりの収入は，去年3.6%上昇した。
UP generate/produce revenue　収入を生む

> **ポイント!** Internal revenue service（国内税収入）は，所得税を集めるところで，アメリカでは，internal revenue を用い，イギリスでは inland revenue を使用する。

188. launch [lɔ́ːntʃ, láːntʃ | lɔ́ːntʃ] v 始める

They have become the first party to officially **launch** their campaign.
彼らは公式に選挙運動を始める第一の政党になった。
UP launch an investigation/career　調査を始める／仕事を始める

189. significant [sɪgnífɪk(ə)nt] adj 著しい，意味のある

The project was launched to deal with **significant** increases in downtown theft.
そのプロジェクトは中心街の窃盗の著しい増加に対処するために始められた。
UP significant difference/effect　著しい差／著しい効果

190. legislation [lèdʒɪsléɪʃən] n 法律

Lawmakers must pass **legislation** that addresses the essential issues.
議員は，本質的な問題を扱う法律を可決しなければならない。
UP enforce/uphold legislation　法律を施行する／法律を支持する

191. nuclear [n(j)úːkliər | njúːkliə] adj 核の

This **nuclear** energy program is a public policy.
この核エネルギー・プログラムは公の政策である。
UP nuclear weapon/power　核兵器／原子力

192. credit [krédɪt] n 税額控除

The law gives taxpayers a **credit** of up to $500 for contributions to private student organizations.
その法律は，私的な学生団体への寄付に対して，納税者に500ドルまでの税額控除を認める。

n 信用貸し

A lower **credit** rating would raise borrowing costs, adding to the country's budget problems.
低い信用等級では，国の予算問題に加え，借用費用を押し上げてしまう。
UP offer/extend credit　信用貸しを申し出る

ポイント！ この単語は，具体的に税金控除を意味する場合と，多くの場合は誰かに貸したお金を意味する。

193. publish [pʌ́blɪʃ] v 公表する，出版する

Justice Scott **published** his conclusions on the sale of arms to Iraq.
スコット裁判官は，イラクへの武器の販売について結論を公表した。
UP publish a book/report　本を出版する／レポートを公表する

194. finance [fɪnǽns, fáɪnæns] n 資金

Check! 50. Her **finances** and credit have also been destroyed, the complaint said.
彼女の資金と信用も台無しにされた，とその原告は言った。
UP public/personal finances　公的資金／個人資金

ポイント！ 単数扱いでも"s"がつくことが多い。

195. source [sɔ́ərs | sɔ́ːs] n 原因，出所

The original **source** of the problem was the failure of the finance minister.
その問題の本来の原因は，財務大臣の失敗によるものだった。
UP locate/track down a source　原因を突き止める

Unit 7

196. compensation [kɑ̀mpənséɪʃən | kɔ̀m-] [n] 補償金，賠償

The woman is accused of illegally accepting workers' **compensation** payments while working.
その女性は，在職中に非合法的に労働補償を受け取っていたと非難されている。
UP award/grant compensation　補償金を与える

197. privacy [práɪvəsi | prív-, práɪv-] [n] プライバシー

The Court must be careful when considering **privacy** expectations in communications made on electronic equipment owned by the government.
政府に属する電子機器で行われたコミュニケーションにおけるプライバシーを考慮する場合，裁判所は注意して取り組まなければならない。
UP invasion of privacy　プライバシーの侵害

198. settle [sétl] [v] 解決する，示談にする

Check! 73. Manila had already **settled** its own claim against the people who control the land.
マニラは，その土地を支配する人たちに対する自身の主張をすでに解決した。
UP settle out of court　示談にする

199. approve [əprúːv] [v] 認可する，承認する

The deal has been **approved** by the boards of both companies and is expected to be settled soon.
その取引は，両方の会社の役員に承認されたため，もうすぐ決着すると思われる。
UP unanimously/overwhelmingly approve　満場一致／圧倒的多数で承認する

> ポイント！ 反意語は，disapprove。

200. impose [ɪmpóʊz | -páʊz] [v] 科す，課す，負わせる

They said it would be a grave injustice for the punishment to be **imposed**.
彼らは，処罰が科せられるのはあまりにも不公平だと述べた。
UP impose sanctions/penalties　処罰を科す

201. survey [sərvéɪ, sə́ːveɪ | səvéɪ, sə́ːveɪ] [n] 調査

In Japan, recent government **surveys** showed more than 80 percent support for the decision.
日本での最新の政府調査によると，その決定を80％以上の人が賛成しているという結果だった。
UP annual/nationwide survey　年間調査／全国的調査

202. obligation [ɑ̀bləɡéɪʃən] [n] 責務

The **obligation** of an attorney is to preserve the privacy interests of those involved in the case.
弁護士の責務は，その事案に関わる人の個人的利益を保護することである。
UP moral/ethical obligation　道徳的責務／倫理的責務

203. threaten [θrétn] [v] 脅かす，脅す

Check! 137. The legislation gives them the power to break up big financial firms if they **threaten** the entire system.
大きな金融会社が全体のシステムを脅かすならば，その法律はその会社を解体させることができる権利を与える。
UP threaten to sue/kill　訴訟を起こすと脅す／殺すと脅す

204. confirm [kənfə́ːrm | -fə́ːm] [v] 確認する

The firm also **confirmed** that the relevant authorities had been notified.
その会社は，関連機関に通知されたことを確認した。
UP confirm a suspicion/hypothesis　容疑を確認する／仮説を確認する

Vocabulary for Law

205. available [əvéɪləbl] adj 利用できる，入手できる

The missing e-mails eventually will be **available** at trial.
その見つかっていないメールは，最終的には裁判で利用できるだろう。
UP easily/readily available　容易に利用できる

206. jurisdiction [dʒʊ(ə)rɪsdíkʃən] n 管区

Can a couple that marries in one **jurisdiction** get divorced in another?
ある管区で結婚したカップルは，ほかの管区で離婚することができますか？

　　　　　　　　　　　　　　　　　　　　n　司法権

The case addresses whether U.S. courts have **jurisdiction** over claims brought by foreign investors who purchased U.S. stock.
その判例は，アメリカの法廷がアメリカの株を購入した外国人投資家による主張に対して司法権があるのかに関して扱っている。
UP claim/exercise jurisdiction　司法権を主張する／司法権を行使する

207. resolution [rèzəlúːʃən] n 解決，決議

He formed a group of former fighters who work for a peaceful **resolution** of the conflict.
彼は，その争いの平和的解決に携わった前戦士たちのグループを結成した。
UP pass/reject a resolution　決議が通る／決議を拒否する

> **ポイント!** この単語はたいていの場合，一般的に「解決」の意味で使用されるが，時に「決議」のように特定の法的意味を表すこともある。

208. proceedings [prəsíːdɪŋs] n 訴訟，法的手続き

Nowadays, we have legal **proceedings** that involve parties located on different continents.
最近，当事者が２つの大陸にまたがる訴訟がある。
UP conduct/initiate proceedings　法的手続きを行う

> **ポイント!** この意味で用いられる場合は，必ず複数形となる。

209. resident [rézədnt] n 住民

Many **residents** complained about loud music at night.
多くの住民が夜のうるさい音楽について不平を述べた。
UP permanent/lifelong resident　長年の住民

210. chairman [tʃéərmən | tʃéə-] n 議長，委員長

The **chairman** of the committee tried unsuccessfully to cap legal fees.
その委員会の議長は，弁護士報酬に上限を課そうとしたが失敗に終わった。
UP chairman of the board　取締役会長

> **ポイント!** 最近では，男性を表す man を用いず，単に chair や chairperson を用いる。

Unit 7

Vocabulary Notes

_____
_____
_____
_____
_____
_____
_____
_____
_____
_____

Make connections between related words (*computer* + *compute*, etc.)

Unit 7 Test Yourself

Quiz 1: Match the words and phrases with their meanings.

1. settle   _____   a. 管区
2. threaten   _____   b. 入手できる
3. survey   _____   c. 判断する
4. available   _____   d. 解決する
5. jurisdiction   _____   e. 弁護する
6. estimate   _____   f. 脅かす
7. defend   _____   g. 調査

Quiz 2: Fill in the blanks with the best word from this unit.

| compensation   residents   publish   revenue   launch   schedule   obligations |

1. Town _____ are very angry with the local government.
2. It's difficult to fulfill _____ to your family when you are busy with work or school.
3. I can't meet you this weekend because my _____ is too busy.
4. When I finish university, I'd like to _____ my own software company.
5. Her dog bit me, so she had to pay _____.

Now check your answers on page 62.

Vocabulary for Law

Unit 8

211. arbitration [ὰɚbətréɪʃən | ὰː-] n 仲裁裁判所
Singapore has become an important venue for international **arbitration**.
シンガポールは，国際仲裁裁判所の重要な拠点となった。
UP go to/resort to arbitration　調停に同意する

212. civilian [səvíljən] adj 民間の
He said he does not recognize **civilian** justice and would only accept being tried in a military court.
彼は，民間司法は認めず，軍事法廷で裁かれることのみを受け入れると述べた。

n 民間人

It is absolutely prohibited to target **civilians** under international law.
国際法により，民間人を狙うことは絶対に禁止されている。
UP innocent/unarmed civilians　無害な民間人／非武装の民間人

213. plead [plíːd] v 主張する，申し出る
A man has **pleaded** guilty to stealing nearly $200,000 from women he met through online dating services.
オンラインデートサービスで知り合った女性から20万ドル近くをだまし取ったとされることに対して，男性は罪を認めた。

> **ポイント！** 他には，plead for help（助けを嘆願する），plead for mercy（慈悲を請う）などのように感情的に訴える表現で使用することが多い。

214. status [stéɪtəs, stǽt-] n 地位，身分，状態
He also emphasized the country's **status** as a world leader in wind and solar power.
彼はまた，風力と太陽光発電の分野におけるその国の世界のリーダーとしての地位を強調した。
UP financial/marital status　財務状態／婚姻関係の有無

215. reform [rɪfɔ́ːɚm | -fɔ́ːm] v 改善する
Academics analyze data about how laws work in order to **reform** the system.
学者たちは，そのシステムを改善する目的で法律がどのように機能しているかについてのデータを分析する。

> **ポイント！** 名詞として使用される場合は，sweeping/radical reform（根本的改善）などとして使用される。

216. traffic [trǽfɪk] n 交通
The plan would help to resolve the city's worsening **traffic** and housing problems.
その計画が，その町の悪化状態にある交通と住宅問題の解決を助けるだろう。
UP air traffic control　航空交通管制

v （不正に）取引する

Those arrested faced charges including arms and drug **trafficking**.
逮捕された人たちは，武器と違法薬物の取引を含む罪に問われた。
UP human trafficking　人身売買

43

217. range [réɪndʒ] v ～の範囲にわたる

The country's consumption of all energy sources, **ranging** from coal to solar power, was equal to 2.265 billion tons of oil.
石炭から太陽光にわたるその国のすべてのエネルギー源の消費は，22億6,500万トンのオイルに匹敵した。
UP estimates/scores ranged from A to B　概算はAからBにわたる／スコアはAからBにわたる

218. ministry [mínɪstri] n 省

Check! 170.
The plan would relocate several government **ministries** outside of the capital.
その計画では，いくつかの省を首都から移動させるだろう。
UP ministry of finance/defense　財務省／防衛省

219. domestic [dəméstɪk] adj 国内の

He agreed that **domestic** law in this regard was missing, though international law did apply.
この点に関しては，国際法には適用するが，国内法においては欠けていると彼は同意した。
UP domestic politics/policy　国内政治／国内政策

> **ポイント！** domestic appliances（家庭用器具）や domestic violence（家庭内暴力）のように家や家庭内のこととして意味することもある。

220. admit [ədmít] v 認める

The singer is facing jail time after he **admitted** to driving while under the influence of drugs.
その歌手は，違法薬物を摂取し運転をしたことを認めた後，収監に直面している。
UP openly/publicly admit　公に認める

221. protest [prətést] v 抗議する

Workers are **protesting** a five percent pay cut ordered by the Madrid regional government.
労働者たちは，マドリッド地方政府からの５％の給与カットに抗議している。
UP strongly/loudly protest　強く抗議する

222. investigator [ɪnvéstəgèɪtɚ|-tə] n 捜査員

Check! 154.
Investigators were considering how a traffic accident could have happened at the boat ramp.
捜査員たちは，船の進水路でどのように交通事故が起こったのか考えていた。
UP private investigator　私的捜査員

223. torture [tɔ́ɚtʃɚ|tɔ́ːtʃə] n 拷問

He was convicted of war crimes, murder and **torture**.
彼は，戦争犯罪，殺人，拷問の判決を受けた。
UP cruel/sadistic torture　残忍な拷問

224. allegedly [əlédʒɪdli] adj 伝えられるところでは

Check! 127.
The hackers **allegedly** destroyed data stored on the card processing network.
伝えられるところでは，そのハッカーたちはカードプロセスネットワークに蓄積されたデータを破壊した。

44 *Vocabulary for Law*

225. convention [kənvénʃən] [n] 条約, 協定

Pakistan is signatory to the Montreal **Convention** of 1999.
パキスタンは，1999年のモントリオール条約に加盟している。
UP signatory to the convention　条約に加盟する

> **ポイント！** political convention（政治集会）のように使用される場合は，大きな集まりを意味する。

226. crisis [kráɪsɪs] [n] 危機

Let's turn the **crisis** into an opportunity for change that has been needed for decades.
この危機を長年必要とされていた変化への機会と捉えましょう。
UP economic/political crisis　経済的危機／政治的危機

227. bomb [bám | bóm] [n] 爆弾

On Monday, a van exploded when it struck a roadside **bomb** in Andar district.
月曜日に，ワゴン車がアンダー地区で側道の爆弾を受け爆発した。
UP explode/detonate a bomb　爆弾を爆発させる

> **ポイント！** 最後の"b"は無声音で，the bomb というと一般的に核兵器を指す。

228. propose [prəpóʊz | -póʊz] [v] 提案する

If I **proposed** increasing their pay, the community would absolutely be angry.
私が給料を上げる提案をすれば，社会は憤怒するだろう。
UP propose a plan/theory　計画を提案する／理論を提案する

229. constitution [kànstət(j)úːʃən | kɔ̀nstɪtjúː-] [n] 憲法, 組織

Check! 186.
There's a debate going on in our country over whether the **Constitution** is going to continue to expand the right to privacy.
我が国で憲法がプライバシー権の拡大を続けるのかどうかに関して議論が起こっている。
UP adopt/establish a constitution　憲法を採択する／憲法を制定する

230. discrimination [dɪskrìmənéɪʃən] [n] 差別

This kind of **discrimination** is something we cannot stand for as a country.
この種の差別は，国として許すことができない。
UP age/racial discrimination　年齢差別／人種差別

231. breach [bríːtʃ] [n] 違反, 穴, 欠陥

The court examined evidence from both sides, and found no **breach** had occurred.
その法廷は，双方からの証拠を検証し，その結果違反は見つからなかった。
UP breach of contract/security breach　契約違反／セキュリティーの欠陥

232. scheme [skíːm] [n] 計画

The **scheme** was set up to reduce the costs of transporting defendants between police stations and courts.
その計画は，警察署から法廷までの被告人の輸送コストを軽減するために作られた。
UP come up with/devise a scheme　計画を立てる

> **ポイント！** 上記の例文のように，一般的な大きな計画の意味で使用される時と，具体的に秘密裡の政治的計画を指す時がある。

Unit 8

233. testimony [téstəmòuni | -məni] n 証言

The trial judge heard **testimony** from the police officer who entered the house.
その公判裁判官は，その家に入った警察官から証言を聞いた。

UP give/offer testimony　証言をする

234. oppose [əpóuz | əpə́uz] v 反対する

He was released by a federal judge, a decision prosecutors did not **oppose**.
彼は，連邦裁判官によって釈放された。それに対して検察官は，反対しなかった。

UP adamantly/vehemently oppose　断固として反対する

235. procedure [prəsí:dʒər | -dʒə] n 手順，手続き

He said prisoners were transferred to Interior Ministry prisons, which was apparently normal **procedure**.
明らかに普通の手順だが，囚人たちは内務省の刑務所に輸送されたと彼は述べた。

UP establish/adopt a procedure　手続きを確立する／手続きを受け入れる

236. testify [téstəfàɪ] v 証言する

Check! 233. Both of them **testified** that they signed the agreement with the hope that their marriage would continue.
2人とも結婚が今後も続くようにと合意書にサインをしたと証言した。

UP testify under oath　宣誓して証言する

237. analyst [ǽnəlɪst] n アナリスト，分析者，解説者

Many **analysts** believe the government continues to maintain links with the Taliban.
多くのアナリストは，政府がタリバンとの繋がりを維持していくと信じている。

UP financial/political analyst　財政アナリスト／政治アナリスト

238. principle [prínsəpl] n 原則，信条

One of the greatest **principles** in the history of cultures is the right to believe whatever you want.
文化の歴史における偉大な原則の1つは，自分が信じるものに対する権利である。

UP adhere to/stick to a principle　信条を守る

239. estate [ɪstéɪt, es-] n 地所，財産

The auction features items which once belonged at the family's country **estate**.
そのオークションは，かつてその家族の地方の地所にあったものを扱っている。

UP real estate　不動産

> **ポイント！** 上記の2つの意味のほかによく使用されるものとして，Her estate can proceed with its case. のように，財産管理人の意味で使用されることもある。

240. reasonable [rí:z(ə)nəbl] adj 合理的な，もっともな，適当な

This law requires officers to question a person's immigration status if there's a **reasonable** suspicion that they are here illegally.
不法滞在しているという合理的な疑いがあるならば，この法律は，移民の身分に関して役人が質問をすることを義務づける。

UP reasonable doubt/expectation　もっともな疑い／もっともな見込み

Vocabulary for Law

Vocabulary Notes

_____
_____
_____
_____
_____
_____
_____
_____

Try to guess the spelling of new words you hear.

Unit 8 Test Yourself

Quiz 1: Match the words and phrases with their meanings.

1. procedure   _____   a. 原則
2. protest   _____   b. 憲法
3. scheme   _____   c. 拷問
4. domestic   _____   d. 手順
5. constitution _____   e. 国内の
6. principle   _____   f. 計画
7. torture   _____   g. 抗議する

Quiz 2: Fill in the blanks with the best word from this unit.

| civilian   arbitration   reasonable   ministries   testimony   investigators   allegedly |

1. She gave her _____ in court, but the jury didn't believe her.
2. It might be difficult to become a _____ again if you've been in the army for a long time.
3. _____ are searching the crime scene right now.
4. My company and I can't agree on my job conditions, so we may have to go to _____ to resolve the problem.
5. That's a _____ idea. Let's try it!

Now check your answers on page 62.

Unit 8   47

Unit 9

241. fine [fáɪn] n 罰金

He could face a year in county jail and various **fines**.
彼は，１年の刑期と様々な罰金に直面するかもしれない。

UP impose/issue a fine　罰金を科す

242. petition [pətíʃən] n 嘆願書

Baraban said that he would file a **petition** for a rehearing.
バラバンは，再審理のための嘆願書を提出するだろうと述べた。

UP file/present a petition　嘆願書を提出する

> **ポイント！** 例文のようにこの単語は，法に関する正式な要求を求めるものに対して使用される。しかし，役所や政府に対して大勢の人が署名した要求などを指し示すこともある。

243. requirement [rɪkwáɪəmənt] n 必要条件

Check! 30.
It is not a **requirement** for the prosecution to prove that the boys knew what they were doing was seriously wrong.
検察にとって，その少年らが自分達の行っていたことがゆゆしき行為であると認識していたと立証することは，必要条件ではない。

UP satisfy/fulfill a requirement　必要条件を満たす

244. attorney general [ətə́ːni | ətə́ː-] [dʒén(ə)rəl] n 法務長官

Check! 8.
His client is pleased that the **attorney general** decided not to bring any action against him.
彼のクライアントは，法務長官が彼に対して訴訟を起こさないと決めたことで喜んだ。

245. bankruptcy [bǽŋkrʌp(t)si, -rəp-] n 破産

Although papers filed in a **bankruptcy** case are public records, the **Bankruptcy** Code recognizes there are exceptions.
破産を宣言した事案は公の記録に残るが，連邦破産法には例外も認めている。

UP declare/go into bankruptcy　破産を宣言する

246. advise [ədváɪz] v 忠告する，勧める

The defense team had agreed with our approach and **advised** him to plead guilty.
弁護団は，その方法で納得し，彼に罪を認めるように忠告した。

UP strongly advise against　～しないよう強く忠告する

247. tribunal [traɪbjúːnl] n 裁判機関

The database could help lead to more investigations in various **tribunals** and criminal courts.
そのデータベースは，様々な裁判機関や刑事事件においてより多くの捜査に導いてくれるだろう。

UP military tribunal　軍事法廷

> **ポイント！** この単語は，多くの裁判官が関係する裁き（審理）の場を指す。

248. verdict [vɚ́ːdɪkt | vɔ́ː-] [n] 評決，判断

His client and the plaintiff both broke down in tears when the defense **verdict** was read.
彼のクライアントと原告の2人は，その弁護評決が読まれた時に泣き崩れた。
UP arrive at/reach a verdict 判断にたどり着く

249. mortgage [mɔ́ːɡɪdʒ | mɔ́ː-] [n] 抵当，住宅ローン

Our crackdown on **mortgage** fraud continues in our campaign against financial crime.
抵当詐欺に関する我々の取り締まりは，引き続きキャンペーンの中で金融犯罪に対して行われる。
UP take out a mortgage ～住宅ローンを受ける

> **ポイント！** "t" は無声音で，発音されない。

250. resolve [rɪzɑ́lv | -zɔ́lv] [v] 解決する

Check! 207.
The quicker we can get those serious issues **resolved**, the better it is for the public.
より早くその重要課題を解決することが，社会のためとなる。
UP resolve a conflict/problem 問題を解決する

251. weapon [wép(ə)n] [n] 武器

This scanning system is designed to detect small **weapons** and metal objects.
このスキャンシステムは，小さな武器や金属製品を発見するために作られた。
UP carry/brandish a weapon 武器を携帯する／武器を誇示する

252. recall [rɪkɔ́ːl] [n] リコール，（欠陥商品を）回収する。

Michigan's attorney general asked Toyota to submit information on the recent U.S. **recalls**.
ミシガンの法務長官は，トヨタに対して最近のアメリカでのリコールについての情報を提出するように求めた。
UP product recall 商品のリコール

> **ポイント！** 動詞形は「思い出す」を意味する。The Panamanian ambassador was recalled from Peru. （パナマの大使は，ペルーから呼び戻された。）のように公的に人を移動させる時にも用いられる。

253. engage [ɪnɡéɪdʒ, en-] [v] 関わる

The recorded conversation does not directly suggest that the man had **engaged** in any criminal activity.
その録音された会話が，その男性が犯罪に関わったという直接的な証拠とはならなかった。
UP directly/fully engaged in 直接に関わる／完全に関わる

254. corporation [kɔ̀ːpəréɪʃən | kɔ̀ː-] [n] 企業

Check! 133.
An appeals court has ruled that a **corporation** in bankruptcy cannot terminate its retirees' insurance benefits.
破産した企業は，退職者の保険手当を解約することができないという判決を控訴裁判所は下した。
UP form/set up a corporation 起業する

Unit 9

255. prime minister [práim] [mínɪstər | -tə] [n] 総理大臣，首相

Check! 170.
The **Prime Minister** has already made it clear that the court ruling will not be defied.
総理大臣は裁判所の判決を覆すことができないとすでに明らかにしている。

256. reveal [rɪvíːl] [v] 漏らす，示す

I'd like some suggestions about how to make sure employees aren't **revealing** company secrets online.
従業員が，会社の秘密をネットで漏らしていないかを知る方法についてアイディアをいただきたい。
UP the study/survey revealed　調査が示した

257. debate [dɪbéɪt] [n] 議論，ディベート

The House passed the bill after a brief **debate**.
議会は，短い議論の後，法案を通した。
UP chair/moderate a debate　ディベートの司会をする

258. occur [əkə́ːr | əkə́ː] [v] 起こる

What **occurred** was more serious than what was reported.
何が起こったのかが，何が伝えられたのかよりも重要である。
UP incident/accident occurred　事件が起こった

259. solicitor [səlísɪtər | -tə] [n] 弁護士

Check! 8.
My previous work as a **solicitor** gave me a deep respect for our justice system.
弁護士としての私の前職が，法のシステムについての深い尊敬の念をもたらした。

> **ポイント！** アメリカで solicitor は，市や町を担当する公務員の弁護士を指し，イギリスでは，barrister（法廷弁士）のために準備をする弁護士を指す。

260. adopt [ədápt | ədɔ́pt] [v] 採用する

Several states have **adopted** tougher rules on when athletes can resume play after an injury.
いくつかの州は，アスリートが怪我をした後に再度競技を始める時により厳しいルールを採用した。
UP adopt a strategy/approach　戦略を採用する

261. candidate [kǽndɪdèɪt, -dət] [n] 候補者

The **candidate**'s ability to obtain the support of his or her own government is very important.
その候補者の自身の政府に対してのサポートを得る能力は，非常に大切である。
UP endorse a candidate　候補者を支持する

262. division [dɪvíʒən] [n] 局，部，課

Once a tip is received, attorneys in the enforcement **division** evaluate the information and decide if action is necessary.
ある情報を受けると，施行局の弁護士がその情報の信憑性を確かめ，行動をとる必要があるかを決定する。

> **ポイント！** division は分割できるものを表し，大企業の場合，firm division（部）と department（課）で区別する。

Vocabulary for Law

263. sector [sékɚ|-tə] n 部門

Check! 155.
The results showed that Europe's banking **sector** is strong enough to deal with any future financial shocks.
ヨーロッパの銀行部門は，今後の財政打撃に対処するのに十分に強固であるとその結果は示した。
UP public/manufacturing sector 公共部門／製造部門

ポイント！ この単語は，262番のdivisionに近い意味で，一般的には経済的な意味や都市の一部を指して使用されることが多い。

264. incident [ínsədnt] n 事件

At least five witnesses videotaped the **incident**.
少なくとも5人の目撃者がその事件を録画した。
UP cause/provoke an incident 事件を引き起こす

265. sanction [sǽŋ(k)ʃən] n 制裁

The EU is planning to adopt new **sanctions** against Iran.
EUは，イランに対して新たな制裁を計画している。
UP apply/impose sanctions 制裁を科す

ポイント！ 基本的には，複数形で用いられる。

266. injure [índʒɚ|-dʒə] v 傷つける

Check! 150.
Dozens of protesters and journalists were **injured** as officers cleared the park.
警察がその公園を一掃した時に，多くの抗議者やジャーナリストが負傷した。
UP seriously/critically injured 重傷を負う

267. indicate [índɪkèɪt] v 指摘する，示す

The government **indicated** that the issue of reforming the law would be among the things investigated by the committee.
政府は，法律改正に関する事柄は，その委員会の管轄内にあると指摘した。
UP study/evidence indicates 研究が示す／証拠が示す

268. prior [práɪɚ|práɪə] adj 先の，前に

In a **prior** incident, similarly statements had been posted by members of the group.
先の事件では，似たような陳述がそのグループのメンバーによってなされた。
UP prior to 〜より前に

269. device [dɪváɪs] n 機器，装置

The officers didn't have any electronic **devices** to measure the speed of the car.
警官たちは，車のスピードを測定するための電子機器を所持していなかった。
UP medical/explosive device 医学装置／爆薬装置

270. warning [wɔ́ɚnɪŋ|wɔ́ːn-] n 警告

The court is not going to eliminate the requirement that police officers give suspects a **warning**.
裁判所は，警官が容疑者に警告をあたえるという条件を排除しないだろう。
UP issue a warning 警告を出す

Unit 9　51

Vocabulary Notes

Use new vocabulary in your writing assignments.

Unit 9 Test Yourself

Quiz 1: Match the words and phrases with their meanings.

1. prime minister _____
2. tribunal _____
3. solicitor _____
4. attorney general _____
5. candidate _____
6. corporation _____
7. requirement _____

a. 法務長官
b. 候補者
c. 企業
d. 弁護士
e. 必要条件
f. 裁判機関
g. 総理大臣

Quiz 2: Fill in the blanks with the best word from this unit.

| fines | adopted | sanctions | devices | indicates | injured | occurred |

1. Last year I was _____ very badly in a car accident.
2. The university has _____ a very strict anti-smoking policy.
3. Computers, phones, printers! I have too many _____ on my desk.
4. Many strange things have _____ around here lately.
5. I had to pay more than $500 in parking _____ last year.

Now check your answers on page 62.

Vocabulary for Law

Unit 10

271. activist [ǽktɪvɪst] n 活動家
Animal rights **activists** say bears are not meant to be kept as pets.
動物の権利保護活動家たちは，熊はペットとして飼われるべきではないと主張する。
UP political/environmental activist　政治活動家／環境活動家

272. acknowledge [əknάlɪdʒ, æk-｜-nɔ́l-] v 認める
They **acknowledge** that what they did had been harmful to the community.
彼らは，行った行為が社会に対して有害であったと認めている。
UP openly/readily acknowledge　公に認める／すぐに認める

273. appellate [əpélət] adj 控訴の，上告の
Check! 123. The **appellate** court said it was "troubled" by the severity of the trial judge's verdict.
控訴裁判所は，第一審裁判官の判決の厳格さに「困った」と述べた。

> ポイント！ これは，court of appeals と呼ばれることもある。

274. labor [léɪbɚ｜-bə] n 労働，仕事
The **Labor** Department says the jobless rate rose in 14 states and stayed the same in 18.
労働省は，失業率は14州で上がったが，18州では変化がなかったと発表した。
UP manual/skilled labor　手仕事／熟練仕事

> ポイント！ Labor Party で労働党を表し，イギリスや他の国々でも大きな政党の1つである。イギリス英語では，Labour と書く。

275. assault [əsɔ́ːlt] n 暴行
Their aunt has been charged with two counts of **assault** and is being held at a county jail.
彼らの叔母は，暴行による2件の訴因で訴えられ，郡刑務所に留置されている。
UP aggravated assault　加重暴行

276. cell [sél] n 房，独居房，細胞
He is being tried for the murders of 31 political prisoners who were pulled from their jail **cells** shortly after his military coup.
彼は，軍事クーデターの直後に31人の政治犯を刑務所の房から連れ出し殺害したとして，裁判にかけられている。
UP prison/padded cell　刑務所房／壁にクッションなどを張った部屋

> ポイント！ terrorist cell（テロの小集団）のように，たいていの場合は，大きな集団の中にある小さな集まりを表す。stem cells（幹細胞）も最近では，法関係の中でよく使用されている。

277. emergency [ɪmɚ́ːdʒənsi｜ɪmɚ́ː-] n 緊急，非常
County police received at least a dozen **emergency** calls from cars stuck on flooded roads.
郡警察は，洪水にはまった車から少なくとも12件の緊急電話を受けた。
UP state of emergency　非常事態

53

278. alternative [ɔːltɜ́ːnətɪv | -tə́ː-] n 代案

The court of appeals said the employer should have considered **alternatives**.
控訴裁判所は，雇用主が代案を考えておくべきだったと述べた。
UP realistic/viable alternative　実現可能な代案

279. guard [gάɚd | gάːd] n ガード

A security **guard** said that the thieves had pulled up in a red BMW at the rear of the building.
セキュリティーガードは，泥棒たちはビルの裏に赤いBMWを駐めたと言った。
UP national/coast guard　州兵／沿岸警備隊

> ポイント！　prison guard（看守，刑務官）は，イギリス英語では warder や wardress といわれる。

280. plant [plǽnt | plάːnt] v 仕掛ける，仕込む

A local official said the bomb had been **planted** near a shop in the valley.
地方当局は，その爆弾は谷の店の近くに仕掛けられたと述べた。
UP plant evidence　証拠を仕込む

281. pursue [pɚsúː | pəs(j)úː] v 推し進める，追跡する

If governments want to **pursue** those interests instead of human rights, they should at least have the courage to admit it.
政府が人権問題の代わりにその関心事を推し進めるのなら，少なくともそれを認める勇気を持つべきだ。
UP pursue aggressively/doggedly　強引に推し進める／根気よく追跡する

282. appoint [əpɔ́ɪnt] v 任命する

The newly **appointed** culture minister resigned his post for health reasons.
新たに任命された文化大臣は，健康上の理由で辞任した。
UP appointed to a committee　委員会に任命された

283. expand [ɪkspǽnd, eks-] v 拡大する

The food company **expanded** its recall to include eggs from all five farms.
その食品会社は，5つのすべての農場から，卵を含んだリコールを拡大した。
UP expand rapidly　急速に拡大する

284. general counsel [dʒén(ə)rəl] [kάʊnsl] n 法律顧問

Check! 25.
Many **general counsel** say the proposed rule would force companies to reveal critical information.
多くの法律顧問は，その提案されたルールでは，会社が重要な情報を示さなくてはならなくなるだろうと述べた。

> ポイント！　例文のように複数形で使用されても形は変わらない。chief legal officer として使用されることもある。

285. conviction [kənvíkʃən] n 有罪判決

Check! 135.
The 19-year-old was sentenced to 25 years in prison following his **conviction**.
19歳の少年は有罪判決の後，25年の懲役を言い渡された。
UP overturn a conviction　有罪判決を覆す

Vocabulary for Law

286. judiciary [dʒʊdíʃièri | -ʃiəri] n. 裁判官

Check! 109.
The report put forward a range of alternatives which would give flexibility to the **judiciary** when dealing with this matter.
そのレポートは様々な代案を載せていたため，この件に対処する際には，裁判官は柔軟に対応できるだろう。
UP federal judiciary　連邦裁判官

287. seat [síːt] n. 席，議席

Five lower house **seats** remain empty because voting was canceled in five politically unstable areas.
5つの政治的不安定な地域において投票が行われなかったため，5つの下院の席が空いたままとなっている。
UP hold/win a seat　議席を保つ／議席を獲得する

ポイント！ 基本的には議席を表し，最高裁判所や他の形態でも使用される。

288. analysis [ənæləsɪs] n. 分析

Check! 237.
The government statement said **analysis** of water samples so far showed no dangerous chemicals.
政府の発表によると，水のサンプルの分析の結果，今までのところ危険化学物質は発見されなかった。
UP careful/painstaking analysis　慎重な分析

289. penalty [pénlti] n. 罰金

Half a billion dollars is the largest **penalty** ever given to a financial services firm.
金融会社に対する5億ドルの罰金は，過去最高額のものである。
UP death penalty　死刑

290. high court [háɪ] [kɔ́ərt | kɔ́ːt] n. 高等裁判所

Check! 24.
The chief justice of the **High Court** agreed to a government request for a three-week delay.
高等裁判所の主任裁判官は，3週間の延期という政府の要求に応じた。

ポイント！ 国によっては，supreme court が使用される。基本的には，最上位の裁判所を表すが，イギリスでは異なる。

291. custody [kʌ́stədi] n. 収監，拘留，保護

Officers are required to tell suspects taken into **custody** that they have the right to remain silent.
当局は，収監された容疑者に黙秘の権利があることを伝えなければならない。
UP protective custody　警察に保護される

n. 親権

The former couple have been locked in a bitter **custody** dispute in Los Angeles.
前のカップルは，ロサンゼルスで苦い親権争いに陥った。
UP joint custody　共同親権

292. factor [fǽktər | -tə] n. 要因

As a law firm, we looked at **factors** like who has access to our data and what will happen to the data in the future.
法律事務所として，我々は誰がデータへアクセスできるのか，そして将来そのデータにどういったことが起こり得るのかなどの要因を考慮した。
UP contributing/risk factor　寄与要因／危険要因

Unit 10 55

293. license [láɪsns] n 免許，ライセンス

The state law requires officers to ask for a driver's **license** or passport if they suspect a person is not allowed to be in the U.S.
州法で，警察がアメリカへの入国が疑わしいと思われる人物がいた場合，運転免許やパスポートの提示を求めることができる。

UP license plate　車のナンバープレート

> **ポイント！**　イギリス英語では，licence となる。

294. assert [əsə́ːt | əsə́ːt] v 主張する

The plaintiffs **assert** that they have suffered harm as a result of the decision.
原告は，その決定によって被害を受けたと主張している。

UP boldly assert　大胆に主張する

295. submit [səbmít] v 提出する

Medical reports are often **submitted** as evidence.
医療記録は，しばしば証拠として提出される。

UP submit a proposal/application　提案を提出する／申込書を提出する

296. disaster [dɪzǽstər | -záːstə] n 災害

The president appointed him to manage the scheme for fishermen and others affected by the **disaster**.
大統領は，災害によって被害を受けた漁師や他の人たちを助ける計画を進めるために彼を任命した。

UP natural/nuclear disaster　自然災害／核災害

297. affair [əféər | əféə] n 事柄，問題，用務

We're surprised this aspect of court **affairs** has not been more thoroughly examined by the media.
裁判の事柄のこの側面に関して，メディアから徹底的に調査されなかったことは驚きである。

UP foreign/international affairs　外交問題

298. negotiation [nɪɡòʊʃiéɪʃən | -ɡəʊ-] n 交渉

After months of unsuccessful **negotiation** they submitted their dispute to the international court.
数ヵ月にわたる物別れに終わった交渉の後，国際裁判所にその論争を移した。

UP conduct/hold negotiations　交渉を行う

299. terrorism [térərìzm] n テロ行為，テロ

They believe that **terrorism** has to be confronted with close cooperation from the international community.
テロには，国際社会と緊密に協力して対処していかなければならない。

UP combat terrorism　テロと闘う

300. appropriate [əpróʊprièɪt | əpráʊ-] adj 適切な，ふさわしい

If they feel the judgment is wrong, then the **appropriate** action is for the Attorney General to lodge an appeal.
判決が間違っていると思うなら，適切な行動は司法長官に上訴することである。

> **ポイント！**　反意語は，inappropriate となる。

Vocabulary for Law

Vocabulary Notes

_____
_____
_____
_____
_____
_____
_____
_____
_____
_____

Try to guess the meaning of new words before you check the dictionary.

Unit 10 Test Yourself

Quiz 1: Match the words and phrases with their meanings.

1. penalty _____
2. activist _____
3. disaster _____
4. affair _____
5. judiciary _____
6. custody _____
7. plant _____

a. 事柄
b. 裁判官
c. 収監
d. 活動家
e. 災害
f. 仕掛ける
g. 罰金

Quiz 2: Fill in the blanks with the best word from this unit.

| assault   emergency   expanded   appointed   submitted   negotiation   cell |

1. After a very long _____, the parties finally agreed on a new contract.
2. I hit him by accident, but I was still charged with _____.
3. In case of _____, leave the building quickly, but please don't run.
4. After I was arrested, I was held in a very small _____ for two months.
5. We _____ an appeal to the judge, but she rejected it.

Now check your answers on page 62.

Unit 10

Vocabulary Notebook

1. **Your Word**　　　　　　　　発音記号　　品詞　　　意味
　　　　　　　　　　　　　　　　[　　　　　]　☐

例文：
....
訳：
....
UP　　　　　　　　　　　訳：

2. **Your Word**　　　　　　　　発音記号　　品詞　　　意味
　　　　　　　　　　　　　　　　[　　　　　]　☐

例文：
....
訳：
....
UP　　　　　　　　　　　訳：

3. **Your Word**　　　　　　　　発音記号　　品詞　　　意味
　　　　　　　　　　　　　　　　[　　　　　]　☐

例文：
....
訳：
....
UP　　　　　　　　　　　訳：

4. **Your Word**　　　　　　　　発音記号　　品詞　　　意味
　　　　　　　　　　　　　　　　[　　　　　]　☐

例文：
....
訳：
....
UP　　　　　　　　　　　訳：

5. **Your Word**　　　　　　　　発音記号　　品詞　　　意味
　　　　　　　　　　　　　　　　[　　　　　]　☐

例文：
....
訳：
....
UP　　　　　　　　　　　訳：

Vocabulary Notebook

6. Your Word　　　　　発音記号　　　品詞　　　意　味
　　　　　　　　　　　　[　　　　　]　□

例文：
....
訳：
....
UP　　　　　　　　　　　　　　訳：

7. Your Word　　　　　発音記号　　　品詞　　　意　味
　　　　　　　　　　　　[　　　　　]　□

例文：
....
訳：
....
UP　　　　　　　　　　　　　　訳：

8. Your Word　　　　　発音記号　　　品詞　　　意　味
　　　　　　　　　　　　[　　　　　]　□

例文：
....
訳：
....
UP　　　　　　　　　　　　　　訳：

9. Your Word　　　　　発音記号　　　品詞　　　意　味
　　　　　　　　　　　　[　　　　　]　□

例文：
....
訳：
....
UP　　　　　　　　　　　　　　訳：

10. Your Word　　　　　発音記号　　　品詞　　　意　味
　　　　　　　　　　　　[　　　　　]　□

例文：
....
訳：
....
UP　　　　　　　　　　　　　　訳：

Index

A

abuse	116
access	113
accuse/accused	80
acknowledge	272
act	15
activist	271
administration	122
admit	220
adopt	260
advise	246
affair	297
affect	180
aid	108
allegation	127
allege/alleged	42
allegedly	224
alternative	278
amendment	98
analysis	288
analyst	237
announce	111
appeal	14
appellate	273
appoint	282
approach	151
appropriate	300
approve	199
arbitration	211
area	39
argument	66
arm	129
arrest	38
article	89
assault	275
assert	294
associate	112
attorney	8
attorney general	244
authority	23
available	205
award	84

B

ban	91
bankruptcy	245
bar	69
benefit	90
bill	52
block	172
board	100
bomb	227
breach	231
brief	169

C

campaign	179
candidate	261
case	1
cell	276
chairman	210
challenge	64
charge	17
cite	168
citizen	176
civil	55
civilian	212
claim	4
client	16
comment	41
commission	65
commit	130
committee	85
community	74
compensation	196
complaint	58
conduct	70
conference	152
confirm	204
conflict	125
congress	132
constitution	229
constitutional	186
consumer	167
contract	96
convention	225
convict	135
conviction	285
corporate	133
corporation	254
council	95
counsel	25
count	140
county	60
court of appeals	123
create	67
credit	192
crime	27
criminal	31
crisis	226
custody	291

D

damages	37
debate	257
decade	166
decline	61
defend	184
defendant	32
defense	51
deny	81
despite	131
determine	119
device	269
disaster	296
discrimination	230
dismiss	153
dispute	62
division	262
divorce	163
document	47
domestic	219
drug	48

E

economic	72
economy	97
emergency	277
employee	76
enforcement	157
engage	253
ensure	183
establish	138
estate	239
estimate	185
evidence	33
executive	86
expand	283
expert	121

F

factor	292
federal	10
fee	36
file	13
finance	194
financial	50
finding	149
fine	241
firm	3
focus	110
fraud	103
fund	49

G

general counsel	284
global	87
grant	83
guard	279
guilty	99

H

hearing	63
high court	290
human rights	68

I

identify	118

illegal	165
immigration	159
impact	181
impose	200
Inc.	106
incident	264
indicate	267
individual	88
injure	266
injury	150
investigate	154
investigation	82
investigator	222
investor	143
involve	34
issue	7

J

jail	164
judge	2
judgment	126
judicial	109
judiciary	286
jurisdiction	206
juror	160
jury	54
justice	9

L

labor	274
launch	188
lawsuit	44
legal	6
legislation	190
liability	162
license	293
litigation	46

M

major	102
majority	145
material	171
media	77
medical	144
military	59
minister	170
ministry	218
mortgage	249
motion	142

N

negotiation	298
nuclear	191

O

obligation	202
obtain	174
occur	258
oppose	234
organization	79

P

panel	71
partner	11
party	19
patent	92
penalty	289
petition	242
plaintiff	22
plant	280
plead	213
policy	35
potential	161
practice	21
prime minister	255
principle	238
prior	268
prison	56
privacy	197
procedure	235
proceedings	208
process	45
project	136
property	120
propose	228
prosecution	134
prosecutor	43
protest	221
provision	173
publish	193
pursue	281

R

range	217
rate	78
reasonable	240
recall	252
reform	215
region	146
regulation	158
reject	94
release	28
require	30
requirement	243
resident	209
resolution	207
resolve	250
respond	147
response	128
reveal	256
revenue	187
role	104
rule/ruling	5

S

sanction	265
schedule	182
scheme	232
seat	287
secretary	178
section	155
sector	263
security	18
seek	20
senate	156
senior	115
sentence	40
serve	105
settle	198
settlement	73
significant	189
site	93
solicitor	259
source	195
spokesman	114
statement	29
status	214
statute	101
stay	141
submit	295
sue	117
supreme court	24
survey	201
suspect	75

T

target	107
technology	139
terrorism	299
testify	236
testimony	233
threat	137
threaten	203
torture	223
traffic	216
treaty	175
trial	12
tribunal	247
try	26

V

v	53
vehicle	177
verdict	248
victim	57
violate	148

W

warning	270
weapon	251
witness	124

Test Yourself – Answer Key

Unit 1	Unit 2	Unit 3	Unit 4	Unit 5
Quiz 1	**Quiz 1**	**Quiz 1**	**Quiz 1**	**Quiz 1**
1. e	1. c	1. b	1. c	1. f
2. f	2. g	2. e	2. g	2. e
3. g	3. a	3. f	3. b	3. d
4. c	4. d	4. g	4. a	4. c
5. b	5. b	5. d	5. e	5. b
6. a	6. e	6. c	6. f	6. a
7. d	7. f	7. a	7. d	7. g
Quiz 2	**Quiz 2**	**Quiz 2**	**Quiz 2**	**Quiz 2**
1. required	1. financial	1. accused	1. aid	1. regions
2. crime	2. alleged	2. executive	2. sue	2. projects
3. clients	3. prison	3. rate	3. council	3. expert
4. firm	4. lawsuit	4. economic	4. contract	4. arms
5. federal	5. arrested	5. settlement	5. banned	5. Despite

Unit 6	Unit 7	Unit 8	Unit 9	Unit 10
Quiz 1	**Quiz 1**	**Quiz 1**	**Quiz 1**	**Quiz 1**
1. a	1. d	1. d	1. g	1. g
2. c	2. f	2. g	2. f	2. d
3. g	3. g	3. f	3. d	3. e
4. f	4. b	4. e	4. a	4. a
5. e	5. a	5. b	5. b	5. b
6. b	6. c	6. a	6. c	6. c
7. d	7. e	7. c	7. e	7. f
Quiz 2	**Quiz 2**	**Quiz 2**	**Quiz 2**	**Quiz 2**
1. treaty	1. residents	1. testimony	1. injured	1. negotiation
2. jail	2. obligations	2. civilian	2. adopted	2. assault
3. obtain	3. schedule	3. Investigators	3. devices	3. emergency
4. citizen	4. launch	4. arbitration	4. occurred	4. cell
5. investigating	5. compensation	5. reasonable	5. fines	5. submitted

著作権法上，無断複写・複製は禁じられています。

Vocabulary for Law　　　　　　　　　　　　　　　　　　　　　　　[B-818]

学問別　重要英単語：法学

第 1 刷　2016 年 3 月 28 日
第 2 刷　2018 年 10 月 17 日

著　者	ラシーン・ジョン	John P. Racine
	中西　貴行	Takayuki Nakanishi

発行者　　南雲　一範　Kazunori Nagumo
発行所　　株式会社　南雲堂
　　　　　〒162-0801　東京都新宿区山吹町361
　　　　　NAN'UN-DO Publishing Co., Ltd.
　　　　　361 Yamabuki-cho, Shinjuku-ku, Tokyo 162-0801, Japan
　　　　　振替口座：00160-0-46863
　　　　　TEL: 03-3268-2311(代表)／FAX: 03-3269-2486

編集者　　丸小　雅臣
製版・印刷　啓文堂
装　丁　　Nスタジオ
検　印　　省　略
コード　　ISBN978-4-523-17818-7　C0082

Printed in Japan

落丁・乱丁，その他不良品がございましたら，お取り替えいたします。

E-mail　nanundo@post.email.ne.jp
URL　http://www.nanun-do.co.jp/